The Norwegian Heritage

The Norwegian Heritage

Arland O. Fiske

North American Heritage Press

International Standard Book Number: 0-942323-12-2

Cover design by
Sheldon Larson of Creative Media, Minot, ND.

Cover photo by
Hruska-Kray-Nauman Photographers, Dubuque, Iowa.

The young girls on the cover are
Anne Marie and Lara Marie Gaylor.

Published by
North American Heritage Press
A DIVISION OF
CREATIVE MEDIA, INC.
P.O. Box 1
Minot, North Dakota 58702
701/852-5552

Printed in the United States of America

Dedication

In Memory of My Grandparents

Ole Olsen Fiske
1869-1929
Emigrated from Surnadal (Romsdal)
to Colfax, North Dakota — 1892

Beret Eggen Fiske
1870-1935
Emigrated from Storen (Trondelag)
to Colfax, North Dakota — 1893

Hellick (Thoresen) Thompson
1859-1931
Emigrated from Lyngdal (Numedal)
to Kassen, Minnesota — 1877

Andrene Bakken Thompson
1871-1954
Whose parents, Ole and Kari Bakken (Hølle)
emigrated from Hemsedal (Hallingdal)
to Blooming Prairie, Minnesota — 1867

They brought the love of Norway and
the Norwegian way of life to America.

CONTENTS

Foreword
Preface

PART I
NORWEGIAN STORIES: ANCIENT AND MEDIEVAL

PART II
NORWEGIAN STORIES: IMMIGRATION PERIOD

x

FOREWORD

THIS COLLECTION OF interestingly-told stories by Arland O. Fiske gives the reader an opportunity to learn of a great many worthwhile things about Norwegians from the ancient time to the present.

A format such as this, with short concise stories, makes it possible for one to pick up the book for a few minutes and be rewarded with a wealth of information served in a delightful manner. Such exposure to a wide variety of topics about the people, places, traditions and history of Norway can very well whet the reader's appetite for a more indepth study of this remarkable "Land of the Midnight Sun."

Mr. Fiske has conveniently arranged these stories in chronological order in three sections: Ancient and Medieval; Immigration Period; and Norway and Norwegians Today. His dedicated research tells us of persons and events of great renown as well as those whose footsteps through the pages of history have not been so well recorded. As we think about who we are, it is well to consider where we have come from. In doing so, we can better appreciate those forebearers in their struggles, their accomplishments, their sorrows and how they enjoyed life.

The Best Of The Norwegian Heritage is a book that spans the ages as well as the continents.

—Sigurd Lindland
General Manager
Norwegian Showcase
EPCOT Center
Orlando, Florida

PREFACE

THE STORIES IN THIS VOLUME, *The Best of the Norwegian Heritage*, have been selected from three previously published books: *The Scandinavian Heritage* (1987), *The Scandinavian World* (1988) and *The Scandinavian Spirit* (1989). Some revisions and corrections were made. The concern in these volumes was to emphasize what Scandinavians have in common. This has been a rich legacy which has bound these people together for a thousand years.

There have, however, come to the publisher many requests for a book of stories which are "strictly Norwegian." They have been grouped into three periods of time. The ancient and medieval period begins with Halvdan the Black (820-860?) and takes us to Prillar-Guri in the early seventeenth century. The immigration period includes stories from the early nineteenth century up to the early twentieth. The third part is about the influence of contemporary Norwegians and ethnic-Norwegians in the world today.

The reader may want to use these stories as an "index" for doing additional reading in the Norwegian heritage. My interest in Norway and things Norwegian goes back to early childhood, even though I didn't get to Norway until fifty years old. It was an emotional experience to set foot on Nordic soil the first time. It still is. I told people I was going to the "holy land," which, in fact, for me it was.

I'm indebted to many people for making this book possible. My wife, Gerda, has been my chief inspiration, together with our children and grandchildren. They share my love of that land and its people. I'm indebted to many friends in the Norsk Høstfest Association, Sons of Norway Thor Lodge 67, and associates in the Scandinavian Heritage Association. Special thanks are due to Allen O. Larson and the North American Heritage Press for making this book possible; to Tammy Wolf for preparing the text for publication; to Sheldon Larson for designing the cover; and to my daughter, Lisa Gaylor, for drawing the illustrations. Thanks to our grandchildren — Anne and Lara Gaylor — for gracing the cover.

I remind you of the motto chosen by King Haakon VII when he accepted the throne of Norway in 1905: "Alt for Norge" ("All for Norway"). There are many of us in the New World for whom these words are still held close to the heart.

—Arland O. Fiske
Minot, North Dakota
May 17, 1990 — Norwegian Constitution Day
"Grunnlovs Dag" (1814)

PART I

Norwegian Stories:
Ancient
And
Medieval

CHAPTER 1

Halvdan
The Black

"HALVDAN THE BLACK" (820-860?) seems a strange name to our ears. Halvdan means "half Dane." His mother, Asa, was a Danish princess. His father descended from the royal Swedish family of Ynglings and was king of Vestfold in southern Norway. He was called the "black" because of his black hair. Not all Scandinavians are blond.

The Scandinavian kings in those days did not live in royal palaces such as the kings of France or Byzantium. They were farmers. The actual farm work, however, was mostly done by women, children, old men and slaves. Raiding, burning and stealing seemed much more fitting for them.

Halvdan's parents had a violent courtship. When his father, Gudrod, lost his first wife in death, he spotted Asa, the beautiful daughter of the king of Agder. His marriage proposal was rejected. So he raided their home, killed the royal family and kidnapped the princess. A year after Halvdan was born, Asa had her revenge. When Gudrod was drunk (drinking was a way of life for Viking kings), she had him murdered, took the child back to Agder and assumed power.

At age 18, when Scandinavians reached legal age, Halvdan claimed both Vestfold and Agder as his territory. It wasn't long before he went on raiding parties and became a "mighty king," according to Snorri Sturluson, the great saga writer.

Queen Asa has been the subject of some interesting speculation. In 1904, the Oseberg Viking ship was discovered in an ancient burial ground southwest of Oslo. It turned out to be the largest collection of objects from the Viking Age ever found in Scandinavia. Two female skeletons were in the royal ship, one about age 20 and the other about 50. It is speculated that the older woman was Queen Asa and the younger was a female slave who was buried with her alive, according to their customs.

The blood of two royal lines, Swedish and Danish, merged in Halvdan the Black. Asa can rightly be called the "grandmother of modern Norway," according to Magnus Magnuson, a popular writer on the sagas. She was the grandmother of King Harald Fine Hair (Haarfagre) who united Norway into a single nation.

Halvdan was considered a wise and just king. He not only made laws, and enforced them, but kept them himself. He came, however, to a tragic death. It was in the spring of the year when he was returning from a feast in Hadeland. Travelling over ice weakened by a late winter thaw, he drowned with all the people in his sledge. During the winter, cattle had been branded on the lake. Some of the dung had eaten through the ice in the warmer weather and it gave way when the king travelled over it.

They were going to bury his body in Ringerike, but the leaders of Romerike, Vestfold and Hedmark demanded equal rights. It was considered good luck for the crops to have a king buried in their territory. So they quartered him and he was buried in four provinces.

Those old pagan times were crude and cruel days. 135 years later, Olaf Tryggvason, a descendant of Halvdan, brought a new religion to Norway. The present King, Olav V, also traces his roots to Asa's son.

The Oseberg Ship.

CHAPTER 2

Harald 'Haarfagre' —
The King Who United Norway

WHEN SELMER NORGARD of Hartland, North Dakota, told me at the Norsk Høstfest that he was descended from King Harald "Haarfagre" (872-930), it opened up quite a conversation. For evidence, his sisters, Helga Anderson of Voltaire, North Dakota, and Grace Brietzke of Minot, North Dakota, brought me the family tree which shows that they are 33rd generation from the famous ruler.

Who was this Harald and how did he become king? He was descended from the royal family of Sweden called the "Ynglings" who claimed lineage from "Yngvi-Frey," one of the Norse gods. At his father's death, Harald became king at age 10 in an area around Oslo.

When Harald became a "Viking," he discovered a beautiful maiden in Valders named Gyda. He sent his men to fetch her for his harem, thinking she would be honored to accept. Gyda, however, was as proud as she was handsome. She said she would not "waste her maidenhood" on a king with such a tiny kingdom and would not even be his wife! She asked why Norway could not have great kings like Denmark and Sweden and replied that she would only marry him if he were ruler of all Norway.

Her arrogance was reported to the king who accepted it as a challenge. He vowed not to cut his hair until he subdued the whole land. He set out at once to conquer every valley and all the coastal regions. It was profitable too, as he demanded taxes and inheritance right from the farmers.

It was no wonder that people fled Norway to settle in Iceland under his rule. Over each of the territories, he set a "jarl" (an earl) to administer his laws and collect taxes. The jarl kept one-third of the taxes out of which he paid his "enforcers." It was so profitable that the politicians of Norway flocked to Harald. They could make more money working for him as jarls than kings had previously made.

Harald's last great battle was at Hafrsfjord, just west of Stavanger. His military campaigns cleaned up much of the piracy that had plagued the coastlands. After 10 years, the battles were won and he turned his attention again to Gyda. But first he got a haircut from his best friend, Ragnvald ("Ronald" in English), Earl of More. The Earl took one look at the king and declared "haarfagre" ("beautiful and thick hair!"). When the messengers came to Gyda the second time, she accepted his offer and bore him five children.

Harald soon became a rich man and added more wives. He divorced nine of them, however, to marry the daughter of King Erick of Jutland (Denmark). She was known as "Ragnhild the Mighty" and had a son known as "Eric Blood-Ax." No one ever accused King Harald of being "soft." Even to his best friends he gave no concessions. Ragnvald's son, "Ganger" Rolf, was banished from Norway for poaching some of the king's cattle. Rolf (Rollo) went on to conquer Normandy in France. Both Olaf Tryggvason and Olaf Haraldsson (the "saint") descended from Harald as does the present royal family of Norway, including Crown Prince Harald.

The next time Norway's royal family comes to the Høstfest in Minot, I hope they will take time to get acquainted with their 33rd cousins.

CHAPTER 3

The Adventures Of
Erik 'Bloodaxe'

THE JUDGMENTS OF HISTORY are still coming in on the Vikings. Historian David L. Edwards, formerly chaplain in the British House of Commons, has written in his book *Christian England* that the Vikings were "thugs" who took advantage of a military vacuum in their times. Emperor Charlemagne had destroyed the once mighty Frisian (Dutch) fleet, but his successors weren't able to maintain control of the seas.

According to Edwards, the Viking terror from the North had as great an impact as the Muslim armies in the south in frustrating the hope that dawned on Europe when the Christian Charlemagne was crowned Emperor in Rome on Christmas Day in the year 800. Edwards wondered that Christian civilization either survived or expanded in those days. Winston Churchill also wrote about those perils in his *History of the English Speaking People*. While Charlemagne lived, he was the protector of Roman Christianity and his enemies kept a safe distance from his armies.

Erik "Bloodaxe" was one of King Harald "Finehair's" nine sons and richly deserved the name "Bloodaxe." Harald was the first of the Norwegian regional kings to gain control over the whole country and Erik was Harald's choice to succeed him. His qualifications included physical strength, a decisive mind, and kinship with King Erik of Jutland in Denmark. He was married to Gunnhild, the daughter of Gorm, the first king to rule over all Denmark. Gunnhild had a reputation for beauty, brains and her father's vengeful spirit.

When Harald died, the struggle for succession pitted Erik against his 15-year-old brother Haakon, who was being brought up in the court of the powerful King Athelstan of England. Erik killed two of his brothers and seemed on the way to seizing control of Norway. A powerful group of farmers opposed him, however, and arranged to have Haakon brought back from England. Unable to stop Haakon's power move, Erik sailed west with his family, ships, wealth, and a small army. After a stop in the Orkney Islands (settled by Norwegians), he went plundering in Scotland and Germany.

In 947, Erik arrived in Northumbria, where a revolution was brewing and the leaders invited him to be their king. They believed that Erik could defend them against the powerful Anglo-Saxon rulers in southern England. A part of the bargain was that Erik and his family had to to be baptized by Wulfstan, the Archbishop of York. Erik agreed, but it didn't change his Viking ways.

The Northumbrians had a stormy history and were hemmed in on all sides by hostile neighbors. They were experienced at playing their neighbors off against each other. Their highways were unsafe for travel, for law and order were not maintained in the countrysides. Travel was risky without armed escort and even then it was considered unsafe to venture more than six miles from home. Foreign merchants brought their wares in by sea.

York, the capital, was an old Roman center, second only to London as a major trading city in the land. More than 30,000 Danes lived in York at the height of its population. Many of the Danes were fourth generation. Second generation Norwegians were there too, as well as other ethnic groups. York, called "Jorvik" by the Norsemen, was also a city of churches with new ones constantly being built.

Today York is a major English tourist center. The Viking-age Jorvik features the restored "Coppergate" section, once the home of carpenters ("koppari"). It's open for tourists throughout the year. If you want information on it, write: Jorvik Viking Centre, Coppergate, York YO1, England. You'll be amazed to discover how authentically the old Viking scenes have been restored.

Erik's first reign in Northumbria lasted less than a year. Before 948 had ended, the Anglo-Saxon King Eadred was back in power. He used terror by sword and fire to break Erik's popular support. He burned Ripon, one of the great cities of Northumbria, including its church. Then he stole the bones of St. Wilfrid, the local saint, to deprive the rebels of heaven's assistance. In the meantime, Erik went "viking" for the next four years. The sagas tell how he ravished the coastlands of Scotland, the Hebrides, Wales and Ireland. His major pirate activity seems to have been in slave trade with the Spanish Moslems. He probably cooperated with the Norwegians in Ireland who made a major business of slave traffic at Dublin.

Slavery was the most profitable business in peacetime for the Vikings. They raided the major church festivals crowded with pilgrims. Ireland, being the most Christian of the North Sea lands, was particularly victimized. The Viking slave traders also covered the markets of Italy, Germany, France and eastern Europe, however. Many captives were delivered to Spain, from where some were sent to the Middle East, others to the Far East. The men were forced into military service or work brigades and the women either became domestic servants or were put in harems. Few of the kidnapped people ever saw their homelands again. It was such a good business that the Spanish Moslems sent representives to Scandinavia to contract for a continual supply of slaves. One shipment saw 9,000 Italians being sent off to Egypt. "Blue men," as the Africans were called, were also sold in the northern lands as slaves.

Erik returned to Northumbria in 952 and was again invited to be king. He defeated a combined English and Scottish army, though at heavy cost. Then he appeared as a pious Christian monarch paying homage to the shrine of St. Cuthbert. His strongest supporter was Archbishop Wulfstan who opposed Anglo-Saxon rule. The Archbishop was captured by the Anglo-Saxons, however, and imprisoned. Erik never succeeded in consolidating his power and was not able to control the seaways. As a result, his second reign lasted for only two years.

A dreadful battle took place between Erik and his enemies in 954 and he and all his men lost their lives. Treachery played a role in his defeat: he was betrayed by the son of a Norwegian-Irish king named Olaf. After his death, Archbishop Wulfstan was set free and restored to power. Despite his ecclesiastical title, he governed much more in the style of a secular ruler than as a servant of God.

Erik's spirit did not end with his death, for Gunnhild and her sons carried on his pirating activities. This also provided an excuse for Gunnhild's brother, Denmark's King Harald "Bluetooth," to renew his military operations in southern Norway on behalf of his nephews.

For all his crudeness, Erik must have had some popular appeal. When he died, Northumbrian writers were kind to his record. A later poet wrote a special story about how Erik entered Valhalla, the hall of the gods, as one of their greatest heroes: "Hail to you Erik, be welcome here and come into the hall, gallant king!" Eulogies still make interesting reading. It just depends on who writes them.

CHAPTER 4

King Olaf
Tryggvason

BEFORE WE JUDGE THE MAN, we should ask about the boy. This is especially true in the case of Olaf Tryggvason (968-1000), king of Norway from 996 to 1000. He was ruler for only four years, but left his mark on the nation forever.

Olaf's father, Tryggve, king of a small area, was murdered by a relative in a power struggle. His mother, Astrid, fled for her life to Sweden, pursued by enemies. Olaf was born on the journey. Finding that they were not safe in Sweden, Astrid set out for Russia with Olaf (now three) to a relative in the service of King Vladimir (Valdemar) at Kiev.

Attacked on the way by Vikings from Estonia, Olaf was kidnapped and sold as a slave. Six years later, an older cousin in the employ of the king spotted him in a marketplace and bought him. Olaf grew up tall, powerful and handsome. In a few years, he was an officer in the Russian army. The other officers, however, became jealous of his popularity and rapid promotions. Realizing his danger, Olaf left Russia. To conceal his identity, he called himself "Ole" and told people that he was Russian.

By age 20, Olaf was a full fledged Viking and ravished the coastlands of England, Scotland, Ireland, Wales and France. On one of these excursions, he was wounded and requested baptism for himself and his warriors. Being zealous for his new faith, he became an eager "missionary." Wherever he went, clergy and teachers went with him.

After spending some time in Christian England, Olaf returned to Norway with a small fleet. He built a church on Moster Island, near Bergen. It's the earliest Christian site in the country. His terms to the pagan Norwegians were: "Be converted or die and have your homes burned!" This was the style of Christian kings in the Middle Ages. Pagan kings didn't give any choice.

NORWEGIAN STORIES: ANCIENT AND MEDIEVAL

In the Trondheim harbor, there is a small island called Munkholmen. Olaf impaled the heads of the pagan rulers on its beach and warned that the same would happen to all if they were not baptized. They complied and elected him king in 996. Being a great grandson of King Harald Harfagre, they quite willingly followed him. Olaf founded Trondheim, called "Nidaros" in those days.

Olaf's undoing came when he proposed marriage to the widowed Queen Sigrid of Sweden, nicknamed the "haughty." They agreed on all the terms except one. She refused to accept his religion. Finally Olaf lost his patience and said, "Why should I care to have thee, an old faded woman, and a heathen bitch?" He angrily struck her in the face. (What a courtship!) Her parting words were, "This may well be thy death."

Sigrid had her revenge. She had Olaf ambushed at sea. Rather than become a prisoner and be tortured, he lifted his shield above his head and sank beneath the waves. He was only 32, but Norsemen still sing his praises. Olaf's statue stands atop a tall pillar in Trondheim's city square. I still feel Olaf's presence when I visit this ancient capital. There is a lesson in this story. The violence experienced by the boy, finds expression in the man.

CHAPTER 5

'Munkholmen' In The
Trondheim Harbor

S TANDING HIGH ON A PILLAR in the center of Trondheim's
business district is a statue of King Olaf Tryggvason. He founded the city about A.D. 996 when the assembly ("Thing") chose
him to be king over all Norway. Out in the harbor, under Olaf's
watchful eye, is a little island which has been witness to much of Norway's history.

The island is called "Munkholmen." When Olaf clashed with the
pagan Norwegians in the area, he hung the head of their leader, Earl
Haakon, on the gallows as a warning to all the people on shore that they
should not resist his new Christian rule. At that time, Munkholmen was
used as a place of executions. His statue has Earl Haakon's head by his
feet.

In 1105, Benedictine monks built a monastery on the island. That is
why it's called "Munkholmen" ("Monk Island") to this day. It was one
of 35 monasteries built in Norway. Monasteries and cathedrals became
centers of wealth in those days, accumulating large tracts of land for
farming. It remained a home for monks until 1531, when the Reformation came to Norway.

In later years, the Danish government used the island as a military
fortress and as a prison for enemies of the king. One such prisoner was
Peter Schumacher, a brilliant young man of German background who
rose to great power in the kingdom. He was known as "Count Griffenfeld." Power, however, went to his head. He was loyal to King Christian V (1670-1699), but the nobles were jealous of him. Because he opposed a war with Sweden, he was branded a traitor and brought to the
place of execution. The gallows were ready and the axe was raised. Then
came the king's reprieve and he was sent to prison, first in Copenhagen
for four years and then to Munkholmen for 18 years.

I listened to the guide tell Griffenfeld's story. At first, he had been
allowed to read and write. When pen and ink were taken away, he tore

bits of lead from the windows and wrote comments on the margins of books. It must have been a cold, damp and lonely place. His health totally broken, he was released in 1698, but died the following year at age 64.

During World War II, the Nazis mounted anti-aircraft guns on top of the ancient castle. It gave me an eerie feeling to stand where Nazi gunners had stood and to realize that they controlled the shoreline all the way from the northern tip of Norway to Africa during my high school days.

Today, Munkholmen looks like the most peaceful place in the world. It's a tourist attraction where you can buy a lunch and stroll around in perfect ease. You can walk the steps of the castle from its dungeon up to the turret. If you ever visit Trondheim, get on a ferry boat and visit Munkholmen. Then let your imagination enjoy itself. You may see King Olaf Tryggvason, the Benedictine monks, Count Griffenfeld and even the Nazis. And if you ever make such a trip, I hope it will be a sunny day for you like it was for our family. It's a place and a story that you will never forget.

CHAPTER 6

Celebration On
Moster Island

MOSTER IS JUST ONE OF 904 ISLANDS in the area called "Bomlo," located south of Bergen. It's a paradise for tourists, featuring boating, fishing and hiking. It's a place of magnificent beauty. We travelled through these waters in the summer of 1984.

Moster claims fame above the other islands as the place where Olaf Tryggvason landed at the port of Teigland in 995 with Viking warriors to begin his conquest of Norway. Here he held the first Christian worship in Norway. From there he sailed to Trondheim.

About 30 years later, in 1024, another Olaf (the "saint") visited the island to hold a constitutional convention for Norway. He wanted to make sure that the Christian faith was established in the land. The new law read: "The first commandment in our legislation is that we shall bow toward the east and pray to the Holy Christ for peace and a fruitful harvest and that we may keep our country settled and tilled and that our sovereign lord (King Olaf) may have strength and health; may he be our friend and we his friends, and may God be a friend to us all."

The church on Moster Island is the birthplace of the church of Norway. Olaf sent one of his clergy, Grimkell, whom he brought from England, to Bremen in Germany to receive consecration as bishop. He believed it would improve his political position if he was on closer terms with the authorities in Rome. The Bremen connection turned out to be useful. Adam, the archbishop of Bremen, was one of the best historians of the time. From him, we learn how both English and German missionaries worked together to make Norway Christian.

The church buildings used to be places of worship for the "glory of God," rather than for the edification of the worshippers. Instruction, sermons and fellowship, as we are accustomed to in America, were not a part of church life. The essential activities were done by the clergy with the people as spectators rather than as participants.

Christianity among the Norsemen was not a religion of love and compassion. Christ was seen as an heroic conqueror who saved the world when he, as "God Almighty," courageously mounted the cross in the sight of all men. It was courage and not compassion that won the Vikings to the new faith. The cross was seen as the ultimate sign of courage.

The people of Moster celebrate their heritage each year with a theatre production called "Kristkongane pa Moster" ("Christ the King at Moster"). The production is directed by Ragnhild Randal, whose husband, Haakon, was President of the Norwegian parliament and is now governor in Bergen. The Randals made a big hit with Americans in 1984 when they attended the Norsk Høstfest in Minot, North Dakota.

The play traces the history of the church from Olaf Tryggvason to Olaf Haraldsson. It tells how the people accepted the faith, then backslid and were finally won over permanently. The music used in the theatre can be traced to those original days. Instruments include medieval lyres, wooden shepherd's horns and trumpets made from goats horns. If you get to Bergen, try to get over to Moster.

L. Gaylor

CHAPTER 7

'St. Olaf' —
Norway's Best Remembered King

W HEN I FIRST LEARNED the nursery rhyme, "London bridge is falling down," I had no idea that it was about Norway's most famous king. He is best known to us as "St. Olaf" or "Olaf the Holy" (Heilige Olaf). He had other names too: Olaf II, Olaf Haraldsson and Olaf the Stout or Thick. What is the connection between this Olaf and the London bridge? And why has his fame survived?

Olaf Haraldsson, who ruled from 1014-1028, was Norway's second king by that name. The first was Olaf Tryggvason (995-1000). The present king of Norway, Olav V, is descended from this line. The "Olafs" (now spelled "Olav") came from a Swedish royal family called the "Ynglings." They entered Norway shortly before the Viking Age (793-1066). The first king to claim rule over all Norway was an Yngling, Harald Finehair, about 890. Olav V also traces his ancestry to Gorm, the founder of Denmark's royal family who lived about 940.

Olaf Haraldsson's father descended from Harald Finehair, but he died quite young. His mother remarried a farmer-king named Sigurd Syr. Olaf was not a model child, unless one should be thinking of a young "Viking." He was pagan in all his ways and showed little respect for his foster father. He was of average height but was very stout. He had medium brown hair and eyes that no one could face when angry. He also excelled in athletic contests and in oratory.

Olaf was only 12 when he went with an uncle on his first Viking cruise. He was especially hostile to the Swedes because they had killed his father. Olaf's craving for adventure brought him to England and to service under King Ethelred. There he fought against the Danes who controlled London and most of England. During an attack on London, it was his idea to fix grappling hooks on the piers which held up the London bridge. His rowers pulled hard and the bridge collapsed. London, however, remained with the Danes.

17

With just 120 followers, Olaf invaded Norway in 1014. He had swift success. Many joined him because he had descended from King Harald. His chief opposition came from the large landowners (bønders) who were against a centralized government. But Olaf outwitted them in both battle and diplomacy.

During a stay in Normandy, a part of France settled by Scandinavians, Olaf became a Christian and was baptized. He took his conversion seriously and became a relentless missionary. Charlemagne (d. 814), the Christian emperor of France, was his model for a ruler. Like his hero, Olaf employed non-compromising methods of evangelism. First, he would speak gently to the people, imploring them to leave their idols and to believe in Christ. Then he invited them to be baptized. But he was firm in demanding decision. He warned them that if they refused they had three choices: Go into exile, become slaves or face him in battle. In a short time, Norway became a part of "Christendom." Clergy from England accompanied Olaf to instruct the people.

King Knut (Canute), the Danish ruler of England, forced Olaf into exile with the Viking rulers of Russia in 1028. Two years later, Olaf hastily returned wih a small army to reclaim his kingdom. He expected that people would join him in rising up against the Danes. King Knut, however, made many promises and most of the farmers marched against Olaf.

On July 29, 1030, Olaf met the enemy at Stiklestad, north of Trondheim. By this time, he had changed in many of his ways. He no longer burned the homes of his enemies, as was the custom. He listened to the reading of the Bible and partook of Holy Communion every morning. But on the day of battle, he was greatly outnumbered. The swords began to clash at noon and by three o'clock Olaf lay dead. His friends secretly buried his body in Trondheim, called Nidaros.

Many people claimed that the dead Olaf performed miracles for them. Even those who struck his death blows praised his virtues. Olaf had become a folk hero against the broken promises of King Knut. A year later, Bishop Grimkel examined the corpse of Olaf. When he opened the coffin, "there was a delightful and fresh smell...his cheeks were red...his hair and nails had grown." Live coals did not burn his beard. Both bishop and the "things" (the ruling councils) were convinced that Olaf was "holy." They did not wait for approval from church authorities in Rome. The Norwegians knew a saint when they saw one. His body was moved to the spot where Norway's national cathedral stands today near the Trondheim harbor. This is also where Norway's kings are consecrated today.

A few years ago, I visited with a pastor from Norway. He was interested in my family name because it originates from a valley southwest of Trondheim. He asked: "Did you know that the Fiske farmers fought at Stiklestad?" In surprise, I said, "Really?" "Yes," he replied, "but they fought on the wrong side."

CHAPTER 8

Harald 'Hardrada'
Returns

HARALD SIGURDSON, known as "Hardrada," was the greatest of all the Viking warriors. And if he had not been caught napping in the sun, the history of the western world may have been quite different.

Harald was the younger half-brother of St. Olaf. On July 29, 1030, when Olaf died at Stickelstad, Harald was just a boy. Against Olaf's wishes, he laced his sword to his arm and joined the fight. Harald suffered serious wounds and escaped to recuperate with the ruling Scandinavian family at Kiev in Russia.

It was not long before Harald was in Constantinople with 500 warriors as the famed Varangian Guard, in the service of the Emperor. They have been called the "Viking Foreign Legion." This was a Viking's delight. He was involved in brave exploits and gathered quite a fortune through the booty that he collected. The Empress, however, began to suspect that Harald was cheating on the Emperor's share and that signalled his return to Kiev where his loot was stored. Before departing, they attacked the palace and put out the Emperor's eyes.

After a brief stay with Prince Jaroslav, the Swedish ruler of Russia, and marrying his daughter, Harald returned to Norway. His nephew, Magnus, son of St. Olaf, had become king. They made a deal to share the power. Then Magnus conveniently died and Harald became undisputed ruler of the land.

Harald was a large and powerful man. Some say he was seven feet tall. At this time, the king of England (of Viking descent) died. Harald Godwinson, a grandson of a Viking, assumed the rule. The Norwegian Harald, who had earned the title "Hardrada" in Norway (which means "ruthless" or "hard ruler"), laid claim to England. He gathered a powerful force and conquered the northeastern part of the country. He felt safe since Godwinson was awaiting an invasion by Duke William of Normandy in the southeast.

It was on the 24th of September 1066 that "Hardrada" was resting in the warm sun with his forces by Stamford Bridge, over 10 miles from their boats. All of a sudden Godwinson's army appeared. It was too late to retreat and this was not the Viking style anyway. Without armor, they plunged into battle. The Norwegians did remarkably well until Harald was killed. Then the slaughter began. All the English soil he gained was the seven feet that Godwinson had promised him for his burial. It was a terrible Viking defeat and was the last time they launched an invasion against England.

If, however, "Hardrada" had been ready, we can only guess what success he would have had against William's disciplined, well equipped and battle ready forces. But supposing that "Hardrada" had won, our lives would have been drastically changed. England would have come under Norwegian rule instead of French. It's true that the "Normans" were Scandinavians, but they had adopted the French language and customs. Then the spelling of English would have been quite different. Who knows, "Old Norse" might have been the official language of the United States today. The Battle of Hastings, however, which took place 20 days later on Oct. 14 changed that forever.

CHAPTER 9

Kaare
Of Gryting

I HAD PAID LITTLE ATTENTION to "Kaare of Gryting" ("gritting") when I first read Snorri Sturluson's "Sagas of the Norse Kings." It wasn't until I visited my cousin, Kaare Rogstad in Orkdal, that I became interested in this little known king. Cousin Kaare, the "sogneprest" (head pastor) of the valley, showed me a Viking pillar with an historical marker by his parsonage that remembers a battle fought over a 1000 years ago. It took place on the fields behind the farm buildings owned by the church.

When I got back from Norway, I took another look at what Snorri had written. It so happened that another Norwegian king, Harald, decided to add to his harem a beautiful and proud young princess named Gyda. She sent word to Harald that she would not even be "honorably" married to him unless he were king over all Norway and not just a few counties. Up to that time Norway had many kings at the same time, each ruling over a small area.

The refusal of the young maiden challenged Harald and he made a vow to the pagan gods that he would not cut his hair until he had brought all Norway under his rule. One of the first places he attacked was Orkdal where Kaare of Gryting was king. Most of the Orkdal soldiers were killed, but he spared Kaare on condition that he would serve Harald. This seemed better to Kaare than death.

It took Harald ten years to fulfill his vow and his hair was pretty long when he went to the barber for a trim, after which the barber called him "Haarfager" (fine hair). That was a safe thing to say. Harald established the Norwegian dynasty which still lives in the present king, Olav V.

Harald appointed Kaare an "enforcer" to collect taxes. It turned out very profitable for him and he became an even more important man than he had been before.

Snorri tells of how Kaare of Gryting opposed the effort of King Haakon the "Good" to make Norway Christian. He was one of eight men who vowed to root out Christianity in Norway and to force the king to sacrifice to the gods.

Years later, when King Olaf Trygvasson forced Christianity on Norway, Kaare was still a power in the community. Olaf threatened to sacrifice him along with some of other leaders to the gods "for peace and for a fruitful season." The result was that all of them consented to be baptized into the Christian faith. The pagan gods had few martyrs. From Orkdal, King Olaf went to Trondheim where he smashed the image of Thor and offered the farmers the choice of conversion or battle. They chose baptism and Olaf took many of their sons as hostages so that they would not relapse into paganism.

The old name of the present parsonage in which cousin Kaare lives is called "Gryting." It's a peaceful place today and has some good farming land around it. The present Kaare of Gryting is a very gentle man and is highly respected in that part of Norway, serving as the "Prosti" or Dean of the pastors.

The days of conflict between the old gods and the "White Christ" are long past, but not forgotten. The record is written in stone.

CHAPTER 10

The Stave Churches
Of Norway

THERE IS NOTHING SO NORWEGIAN as a stave church, not even lutefisk. Once there were over 1000, today there are only about 30. They can be found as far north as the Folk Museum in Trondheim and as far south as Telemark. These churches were built between the 11th and 14th centuries, almost all before the "Black Death" which struck Norway in 1349.

These timbered structures were built around huge poles planted into the earth and made their appearance about the same time as Christianity entered Norway. The first ones rotted away, but later churches built on sills and beams have survived to this day.

The designs of the stave churches are both ingenious and beautiful. Timbers were selected for size and strength in the days before Norway's forests had been exploited. They are called "stave" churches because of the heavy corner posts and wall planks. When a tree was selected, its branches were trimmed off except for the very top. In this way the tree would die slowly and the lumber would cure. This is why some are still standing after 700-800 years.

The earliest stave church is in the Folk Museum in Oslo's Bygdøy Park. It was moved from Gol in Hallingdal about 100 years ago. Having fallen into disrepair, it is now in excellent condition. The paintings by the altar date from 1652. The "Gol" church has a special interest to me since it was located a few miles from Hemsedal, the home of my earliest family in America who emigrated in 1867.

The largest stave church is called "Heddal" ("Hitterdal") and is located at Notodden in Telemark. It's a huge structure surrounded by a cemetery. It's in excellent condition, having been restored. Both crosses and serpent heads decorate the exterior. The early builders retained some of the images of the pagan past, while committed to the new religion.

It has sometimes been suggested that the architectural design of stave churches resembles the pagodas of Southeast Asia. I asked Kjell

Johnsrud of Notodden about this when he showed me the Heddal church. Johnsrud is an authority on lumber and stave church design, being a lumberman himself. He denied any foreign influence and stated that the pattern was authentically Norwegian for its time and the building materials used.

One of the interesting features found in some stave churches is a little window near the altar. It was used to serve communion to people with leprosy. They were not allowed into the churches but were given the sacrament through this opening. Leprosy was a major health problem in western Norway in the Middle Ages due to unsanitary conditions in the homes. In 1873, Dr. G. A. Hansen, a physician from Bergen, isolated the bacillus. Today Norway is free of the disease.

The oldest stave church which remains almost exactly as built is at Borgund in the Sogn region of western Norway. Constructed about 1150, it is one of the best known of these churches and is often seen on pictures. It is the model for the "Chapel in the Hills" near Rapid City, South Dakota, home of the Lutheran Vespers radio broadcast. Completed in 1969, it's built of fir and cedar and is visited by over 50,000 people each year.

The Hedalen church in Valdres boasts an interesting story of a lost hunter and a bear. During the Black Death, the entire population of some communities was wiped out or people just fled in fear. Years later, a hunter far from home, missed a bird with his arrow and it struck the church bell. After recovering from fright, he investigated and found the lost church and a bear asleep in front of the altar. A bearskin hanging in the church testifies to the tale.

One of the most impressive features of these churches is the wood carvings about the entrances. In some cases, the ceilings are built like the frame of a Viking ship. The origin of these buildings is rooted in mystery, but there is a beauty about them that describes the faith and piety of the people. One tradition tells that St. Olaf made a deal with a troll to build the first one. Whatever it was, they are magnificent structures and remind us of a different Norway than the one we know today.

The stave churches are now a part of Norway's national treasure. If you ever visit this land of the Vikings, don't fail to see at least one of them.

CHAPTER 11

The Cathedral
In Trondheim

NO CHURCH IN THE WORLD is as exciting to me as the Nidaros Cathedral in Trondheim. This is not because it is the largest church in Scandinavia, but because of the story that goes with it. I grew up with a picture of this church in the living room of our farm home.

The Nidaros Cathedral dates to July 29, 1030, the day King Olaf Haraldsson fell in the battle of Sticklestad. Olaf's body was carried 75 miles by friends from the battlefield to the River Nid for burial. Soon people began claiming that miracles were performed by the fallen king. A year later, Bishop Grimkel, declared Olaf to be a saint and martyr. His body was put in a silver casket studded with jewels and placed on the altar in Clemen's Church.

It was not long before Olaf was called "Norway's Eternal King," a title still given to him. On the sight of his burial, a spring of water began to flow and people came to it for healing, according to the saga by Snorri Sturluson. A chapel was built and the altar was placed where Olaf had been buried. Soon a flood of pilgrims from all over northern Europe began trekking to Trondheim, making it the fourth most frequented holy place on the continent.

Olaf's younger brother, King Olaf Kyrre, began building the new Christ Church on the site in 1070. Many fires have ravaged this church, but it has always been restored. The most recent renovation began in 1869. The length of the building measures almost 400 feet. The baroque organ, the largest in Scandinavia, was built in 1930.

The work of many famous sculptors adorns this building. One of these, Gustav Vigeland, is best known for his statues in Frogner Park in Oslo. The husband of a cousin to my father, Stephen Krogstad, spent his entire lifetime making statues for the west wall. He was twice honored by the King for his work.

The greatest feeling for this historic church is experienced through worship. Despite the splendid architecture and furnishings, the liturgical service is quite plain. Even if you know only a little Norwegian, it is not difficult to follow. I timed the pastor's sermon. He used only 11 minutes for the prayer, reading of scripture and the sermon. He spoke very plainly and clearly. There was nothing pompous about it. The sanctuary was fairly well filled, including quite a few young people. The music was outstanding, both the choir and the organ. Concerts and recitals are regularly held in the nave.

Whenever I approach this gray soapstone building, I get the feeling of walking on holy ground. The cathedral towers above all other buildings in the city and can easily be reached by walking from any part of the downtown. A cemetery surrounds it on the north and east.

I have been to Nidaros several times and will be drawn back to it again. Whatever a person may think about the saga accounts of Olaf the Saint, there is a mystique about this place. Even though Olaf's body has secretly been buried somewhere in or near the cathedral and the casket melted down in Denmark, Nidaros continues to cast its spell on all who visit it.

Nidaros Cathedral in Trondheim.

27

CHAPTER 12

The 'Hanse'
In Bergen

I F YOU WANT TO SEE SOME OF THE BEST preserved buildings from the Middle Ages in Norway, go to Bergen. Down by the waterfront, in an area called the "Tyskebryggen" (The German Wharf), stand rows of connected wooden buildings built by German merchants. They have their own special style. As high as five stories tall, they have sharply pitched roofs. Today these buildings house Norwegian shops, but for almost 500 years they represented the dominance of foreign trade interests in Norway.

Bergen is a lovely city nestled around a natural harbor that has been in use for over a thousand years. Even today with all of the modern developments, its natural beauty has been preserved. It is also the largest city in west Norway. I had eagerly looked forward to seeing the museum of the Hanseatic League in Bergen which tells the story of the German period in west Norway.

Bergen was founded in 1070 by King Olav Kyrre to provide a market place for fish and furs. England was its chief trading partner between 1150 and 1250. But then the Germans got interested. In 1294, trade privileges were given to Lubeck, Rostock and other cities of north Germany which made up the Hanseatic League, on condition that they pay tithes to the church.

It began with summer trading, but it was not long before they built permanent year around headquarters. Open clashes sometimes occured between the 2000 foreigners and the local population (5000-8000). The Hanse brought only men and older boys to Bergen and did not fraternize with the people of the city. They were armed. During this time, Norway was weakened by the "Black Death" (1349) and lost control of its coastlands and commerce. The Hanse remained until 1761. In addition to fish and fur trading, they brought many skilled craftsmen to Norway such as tailors, shoemakers, goldsmiths, furriers, bakers and barbers. They also opened up businesses in Oslo, Tonsberg and

Trondheim. The struggle between the Norwegian kings and the Hanse centered in the monopolistic practices of the foreign merchants.

The most famous old church in Bergen is "Mariakirken" (St. Mary's Church). It was assigned to the Hanse in 1408 and regular German services were held in it until 1868. It has a high pulpit, sculptures, a hanging ship and is built like a fortress. During the Reformation, the Hanse sided with Martin Luther and brought Lutheran pastors to the Mariakirken in 1526, 10 years before Lutheranism became the established church in Norway.

Did the Norwegians like the Hanse? It was a mixed blessing. The Norwegians needed the foreign capital to develop business. They also needed the craftsmen from the Continent. However, they had one special gripe. The Germans got control over the cod fish trade from the Lofeten Islands which was used for making lutefisk. They shipped most of it back to Germany. You can imagine the physical and emotional suffering this caused the Norwegians. I had always wondered about the unusual appetite that our German cousins have for this "heavenly food" when they attend the Norsk Høstfest in Minot. Now I know. The Hanse started it.

CHAPTER 13

Akershus —
Fortress Of Old Norway

"NEVER CONQUERED," can be said of very few places in the world. This is the proud boast of "Akershus," a fortress of old Norway. The Oslo harbor is dominated by this castle which was the home of many Norse kings and which has protected their people.

An invasion from Sweden in 1287 prompted the building of this fortification. The walls were built 10 feet thick and over 50 feet high. Building began in 1300 and it was none too soon. There was another invasion from Sweden in 1308 by the king's own son-in-law.

Among the interesting royalty to live in Akershus was Queen Margaret I (1352-1412). It was while living in this castle as an 18-year old queen that she wrote to her husband off in battle: "I want you to know . . . that I as well as my servants suffer from great shortages of food." Then she asked for money "so that those who are with me shall not be separated from me for reason of hunger." The letter was written in late fall. In December, she gave birth to Norway's future king, Olav IV. This castle was no haven of luxury, but it did give protection from its enemies. It was beseiged nine times during the four centuries it served as a fort, but it was never conquered. The last attack was in 1716 by another force from Sweden. The cannons drove off the enemy.

For the next 150 years, the building fell into neglect and disrepair. Forgotten as a part of the nation's defenses, it was used to store equipment and grain. It was not until the 1890s that its historical value was appreciated.

Today, Akershus is an impressive and beautiful landmark. The ancient cannons with their red wooden wheels point out over the harbor like they are ready to challenge any intruder. Cast between 1556 and 1572, they were restored in 1962.

Inside the castle are huge halls and a banquet room, which are used for special state functions. There is also a large memorial in granite on the grounds remembering Norway's dead of World War II. The Resistance Museum of that war is also housed within the walls.

At night, the entire castle area is lit up. To visit this fortress of old Norway gives a person a strong feeling for the country's medieval days. A visitor today gets only the impression of peacefulness on these beautiful grounds. But it has not always been so. Many stormy battles and much bravery have been witnessed here. This is also the place were Vikdun Quisling, the pro-Nazi traitor who urged Hitler to invade Norway, was executed. After a trial which received international press coverage, he faced a firing squad on Oct. 24, 1945, almost six months after his arrest.

Akershus is more than a castle. It is a symbol of the mind and will of Norwegians to be free. If you should go to Norway and have never seen it, make sure that you allow time for it. This medieval castle and Renaissance palace will stay in your memory forever.

CHAPTER 14

The Fritjof
Saga

HIGH ON THE MOUNTAIN overlooking the fjord across from Balestrand in western Norway, stands the statue of Fritjof. Not far away on the same height is the statue of King Bele, after whom the beach ("strand") is named. They are looking in opposite directions.

The statues were a gift from Kaiser Wilhelm II of Germany who used to vacation each summer through 1913 at the Kvikne Hotel in Norway's "westlands." This was his way of showing appreciation for the month each summer that he'd spend in this place of unusual beauty.

Fritjof was the son of Torstein, a real Viking who lived on the farm called Framnes (now Vangsness). Interestingly, this was the birthplace of Frederick of Vangsness, great grandfather of Walter Mondale, former Vice President of the the United States. Time magazine carried a story in 1984 which stated that if Frederick had not moved to his wife's farm (Mundal) and taken her name when he got married, that the former presidential candidate would have been known as Fritz Vangsness. Fritz (or, Frederick) is another name for Fritjof.

King Bele and Torstein had been good friends. They lived in the seventh century, 400 years before St. Olaf (d. 1030). He was considered a good king. He warned his sons, Helge and Halfdan, to keep friendship with Fritjof, for the son of Torstein was a mighty warrior.

The King had an attractive daughter, Ingeborg the "fair," the most beautiful girl in the kingdom, known for her golden hair. (At that time, Norway was divided into many small kingdoms.) And since they were both well born, they lived for a time in a foster home where they were educated for their futures. Fritjof and Ingeborg became fast friends. And when the time for romance came into their hearts, they felt for each other. But by this time old King Bele had died and so had Torstein.

Ingeborg's brothers served jointly as kings and refused the warrior's request to wed their sister, saying "Our sister was not for a vassal born. A King's son alone shall Valhalla's beautiful daughter own, but our serf you may be." Despite his wooing and offer to prove his worthiness with the sword, the local assembly ("Thing") agreed that Fritjof should be banished to the Orkney Islands for a year. If he returned with the taxes which the Jarl owed the Vangsness kings, he should have his bride.

Fritjof returned within the year with the tribute from the Orkneys. But alas, it was too late. Another King, Ring from the Eastland, now claimed the hand of Ingeborg. Ring was an older man and mighty in war. When the brothers refused to accept his offer, Ring brought his army to bring her to his farm by force and to the altar of Balder for the marriage rite. (Balder was one of the gods in the Norse pantheon together with Odin, Thor, Frey and others.) Fritjof accepted his fate as the anger of the gods, though he knew himself to be a worthy man and that King Bele had wished him to be his son-in-law. In anger, Fritjof burned Balder's temple.

Then he took to sea in a magic boat named Ellida, which could speak to him. For several years he rode the waves until he could stand it no longer. He returned to King Ring's banquet hall at Juletide, not to claim a bride but to see her just once more. He entered disguised as a "greybeard," wearing a wild bear's skin. But when insulted by a guard, with feat of strength he lifted him high and turned him upside down.

This got the King's attention and he demanded to know who this stranger might be. When he removed his garb, the King and all could see it was Fritjof, the mighty warrior. The Queen's cheeks paled. King Ring, gracious in manner, invited the warrior to spend a year. In the spring, when the hunts began, the King became exhausted and rested with Fritjof as his guard. Fritjof fought the temptation to behead his rival and claim the Queen. Being found faithful, the King made him his "son," and said "Thou seest I am aged grown, and to the grave must soon recline. Then take thou to my realm, and take the Queen for she is thine."

It happened soon afterwards that the old King gathered his friends and in true Viking fashion committed suicide so that he would go directly to Valhalla (the Viking "heaven"). The people quickly elected

Fritjof to wear the crown and wed the Queen. He agreed to be their king, but much to their surprise refused the Queen, saying he would choose his own bride. This was his way of not becoming beholden to them.

While visiting his father's grave to seek wisdom, he was guided by a vision to rebuild the temple of Balder. Soon afterwards, he was reconciled to the sons of King Bele and took Ingeborg to wed. "Ingeborg over Balder's altar gave her hand to him her childhood's friend and her heart's delight." It ended as a hero's story ought. Fritjof won his prize, but only after years of toil and proving himself a worthy man.

There's a lesson in the story. Whatever the prize you seek, first prove your worthiness to possess it. Fritjof still stands guard over the fjord at Vangsness across from Balestrand. The only way to get there is by ferry. I hope you can visit Balestrand some day and wish for you a day of sunshine as it was for us. Take a look at the top of the hill where the Kaiser's gifts still stand. It has become a part of the Scandinavian heritage.

CHAPTER 15

Norse Rune Stones
In America

NOT EVERYONE HAS AGREED with those who delcared the Vinland Map a forgery. One of these was Dr. O. G. Landsverk, a Norwegian-American scientist and former nuclear physicist with a Ph. D. from the University of Chicago. He collaborated with Alf Monge, a former cryptanalyst with the United States Army Intelligence.

If I had any doubts of the competence about these scholars, I was reassured by Prof. H. M. Blegen of Augustana College, Sioux Falls, South Dakota, who has written of them with high praise. Since I've had the greatest respect for Dr. Blegen, I've studied the work of these two scholars with special interest. When Yale University issued its statement in 1974 suggesting that the Vinland Map may be a forgery, Landsverk claimed the tests to be faulty on which the conclusions were based.

Landsverk's book, *Runic Records of the Norsemen in America*, is impressive. His data compares runic writings found in the Orkney Islands, Greenland, New England, Minnesota, Illinois, the Dakotas and Oklahoma. He credits Alf Monge, a specialist in decoding messages for the Army, with having discovered the secret to understanding the runic messages. They note, however, that not all runic writings contain these cryptic insertions.

The Norse presence on the North American continent has been tied to their existence in Greenland from 986 to 1500 A.D. An abundance of Norse artifacts have been found in the New World, but there has been a deep-seated resistance to accept them as evidence. The work of Landsverk and Monge claims to have discovered hidden dates in them from the "Primstav," the perpetual church calendar of the Middle Ages. The announcement of this discovery was made in 1967. I'm not aware that anyone has successfully challenged their claim.

Landsverk was convinced that the Kensington Stone found near Alexandria, Minnesota, which claims to date from 1362, is authentic. He also claims that bones excavated in 1905 from Mandan Indian sites north of Bismarck, North Dakota, have Norse runic inscriptions. Some of these are on display at the Peabody Museum at Harvard University, some at the Smithsonian Institute and three are at the Ft. Lincoln Memorial Museum at Mandan, North Dakota. These finds become especially interesting in the light of Verendrye's observation in 1738 that the Mandan Indians had many European characteristics.

What were those Norsemen doing in Midwest America 500 years before Columbus? Landsverk claims that the ship carrying the "8 Goths and 22 Norwegians," which travelled to Kensington, set sail from Bergen in 1355 by order of King Magnus "to find and bring back to the true faith the Norse Greenlanders who had abandoned their homes in Greenland" and settled on the American continent. He was supported in this theory by the late Hjalmar Rued Holand, professor at the University of Wisconsin.

But how do the runic writings fit into this story? Runic, a form of writing carved into rocks and wood, was used by the Norsemen before Christianity and the Latin took over about 1000. Runic, sometimes called "futhark," continued to survive among the Runemasters, chiefly clergy, who used it to inscribe coded messages.

The runes expressed numbers as well as sounds, according to Landsverk. The Primstav was used by the Norse puzzlemasters who kept on using their runic writing long after it was considered "unchristian" to do so. It's interesting that it was the Norse clergy who became the experts in writing secret messages with runic inscriptions. As a result Norwegian and Swedish churches of the Middle Ages are decorated with runic writings. The Scandinavian church, having originated through England instead of the Continent, seems to have been permitted this deviation from church practice until about 1350 to assure loyalty to Rome. The Norse clergy retained the spirit of freedom which was part of their ancient tradition, a trait still inherent in Norwegian-Americans today. In the 17th century, runes were identified with magic and many people were put to death in Iceland just for having knowledge of them.

The stave church from Gol in Hallingdal was brought to the Folk Museum at Bygdøy Park near Oslo in 1885 with the help of King Oscar II. It has 13 runic inscriptions. Early attempts to read them proved difficult until Alf Monge's work of deciphering. For a while, scholars had thought them to have been done by amateur writers. Not only stave churches, but Nidarosdomen, Norway's national cathedral in Trondheim, has 40 runic puzzles.

Many reports on the Kensingston Stone have commented on its "bad Latin." Later cryptanalysis by Monge claims them to be the evidence of Norse puzzlemasters. The Kensington Stone was discovered in 1898 by Olaf Ohman, a Swedish farmer. Magnus Magnusson, creator the popular "Vikings!" PBS-TV series, has called it a "forgery," together with the Vinland Map. His arguments sound convincing. But I have two reasons, neither of them scientific, for thinking that the Kensington Stone may be for real. First, those Norsemen from the Middle Ages were resourceful travellers. Second, there's a snobbery on the part of many Europeans which is reluctant to admit that anything of importance has happened in the New World. It's still a British inuendo to regard the United States as one of the "colonies."

CHAPTER 16

The Reformation In
Denmark And Norway

THE RELIGIOUS REFORM MOVEMENT that broke out in Western Europe during the 16th century moved in many different geographical and doctrinal directions. While there had been previous attempts to challenge and change the church before this time, none was successful. It was a dangerous endeavor which produced many martyrs. John Wycliffe (1328-84) in England, John Huss (1372-1415) in Bohemia, and Girolamo Savonarola in Italy (1452-98) all experienced the fires of religious intolerance. The age of religious freedom had not yet arrived.

It was in a little back-water city of Saxony in Germany that the unexpected events began that were destined to reshape western society. The movement led by Martin Luther was primarily a religious event, but it touched off a fire that had long been smoldering due to resentment towards the church's vast land holdings and control of wealth, while exempted from taxation. The feudal system also contributed to the repression of the people.

Humanism was another factor that encouraged reform. Renaissance scholarship and freedom of inquiry promoted the study of the Bible in the original Greek and Hebrew texts. Disiderius Erasmus of Rotterdam (1467-1536), a Dutch humanist, scholar and critic, had a powerful influence on the thinking of those times.

Even though Scandinavia was in an area isolated from the mainstream of events, it could not be sheltered from the reform movement of Germany. In Denmark, a Carmelite monk, Poul Helgeson, an admirer of Erasmus, prepared the way for the eventual Lutheran takeover, though that was not his intention. He approved of much of Luther's teaching but did not want separation from Rome. This was the case with many of the reform-minded church leaders.

King Christian II (reigned 1513-23) favored a national church with the king as the head, yet aligned with Rome. It was not uncommon for the king to be in conflict with the nobles and in 1523 Christian was deposed by them in favor of his nephew, Frederick I (reigned 1523-33). Christian went to Wittenberg and listened to the preaching of Luther while staying at the home of Lucas Cranach, the famous artist. Impressed, he commissioned a translation of the Bible into Danish. But since he was a brother-in-law to Emperor Charles V, who thought of himself as the protector of Roman Catholicism, Christian later renounced his Lutheranism in the hope of regaining his throne. He began with an invasion of Norway where he was supported by the archbishop. Defeated, he was arrested and spent the rest of his life in jail.

Frederick remained nominally loyal to Rome but protected the Lutherans and built a theological college at Haderslev which became a center of Danish Lutheranism. For three years (1533-36), Denmark was torn by a civil war. It ended with Frederick's son, Christian III (reigned 1536-59), coming to power. He was a deeply religious man and a practical politician. Recognizing that the bishops controlled most of the nation's wealth, he promptly arrested them and deprived them of their lands and temporal power. A new church constitution (approved by Luther) was adopted, and "superintendents" elected by the pastors replaced the bishops.

In exchange for becoming the head of the church, the king bound himself to worship God and maintain the practice of the Christian faith. This has been done faithfully in Denmark down to the present monarch, Queen Margaret II. The new superintendents (later called bishops again) were ordained by Rev. Jonas Bugenhagen of Wittenberg, a close friend of Luther. Christian III became an absolute monarch and Norway became a mere province of Denmark instead of being a partner in a dual monarchy.

While the Reformation in Denmark involved a lengthy struggle, including a civil war, the religious change in Norway took place by the command of King Christian III. It came at a time when the political, cultural and religious life of the country was at its lowest ebb. The Danish Church Ordinance of 1537 was ratified by the legislative assemblies (diets) in Oslo and Bergen in 1539. The archbishop, Olaf Engelbrektsson, found himself virtually alone in wanting to keep the ties with Rome and fled the country. Most Catholic priests became Lutheran priests (prester), which they are still called. Among the strongest supporters of the Reformation were the priests' sons, for now their parents could be married like other parents and they would become legitimate. It also meant that their mothers would become women of honor instead of privately kept mistresses. (Although celibacy was the rule for the clergy, it had proved to be unenforceable in Scandinavia.)

The first Lutheran bishop appointed to Norway was Geble Pedersson, also ordained by Bugenhagen. While the Reformation was mostly peaceful in Norway, there were places where the people fiercely resisted the king's ordinance. Some of the old church records were burned and religious artifacts identified with the old religion were destroyed. This has been a great loss to genealogical research.

In Denmark, many beautiful wall paintings inside churches were covered with whitewash and are just now being restored. As a result, however, the paintings were also preserved. We saw some of these in a well-preserved church building from the 1200s at Sindal in North Jutland, an ancestral home of some of my wife's family. We also visited some of the old monasteries which still stand but are now used for other purposes. It took about two generations of indoctrination before there was a major change in the piety of the laity. Spiritual reformation did not really come to Norway until the preaching of Hans Nielsen Hauge (1771-1824), a farmer who called the nation to repentance.

As a result of the Reformation becoming a law in Norway, the Danish influence became strong. The Danish Bible, catechism, and other religious books were used. Until 1813, all clergy were educated in Copenhagen. There was not a Norwegian translation of the Bible until after 1814, when Norway came under the rule of the Swedish king. That's why the Bibles and liturgies used by Norwegian immigrants were more Danish than Norwegian.

The Hanse, merchants from Lubeck and other north German cities, were among the earliest to practice Lutheranism in Norway, especially in Bergen. A beautiful church built by the Hanseatic merchants still stands near the harbor in that beautiful city. One of the early effective bishops was Jorgen Eriksson (1571-1604) of Stavanger.

The 16th century was not an easy time in which to live. There were many good people, but intolerance, disease and the social caste system repressed the aspirations and potential of most people while giving opportunity to a privileged few. Still, our ancestors managed to survive. They could never have believed the times in which we live. I'm glad to be living today despite the dangers that surround us.

Martin Luther — reformer.

CHAPTER 17

Lady Inger
Of Austraat

C AN THE INFLUENCE of one person shape a nation and the future generations of its people? Could a woman have such power? Since most historians have been men, it should not surprise us that some outstanding women have gone unnoticed.

Such is the case with Lady Inger of Austraat, who lived north of Trondheim in Norway. She even escaped the attention of the famed Yale historian, Roland Bainton, when writing a three volume work on *Women of the Reformation*. I'm indebted for much of my information on her to Prof. Kenneth Christopherson of Pacific Lutheran University in Tacoma, Washington.

Born about 1475 of a long line of Norwegian nobility, Inger inherited great wealth in money, property and land. Married at age 19 to a famous knight, Nils Henrikson, she became the mother of five daughters, three of whom married Danish noblemen. But it was not until her husband's death, when she was 48, that her genius for power was recognized.

Many, if not most, great events of history cannot be predicted. It often happens that seemingly unimportant circumstances become major happenings. It was such a meeting of occurrences that took place in the 16th century as the Reformation spread from Germany to Norway.

It started in Denmark during the power struggle between King Frederik I, a Lutheran sympathizer, who was struggling to establish his rule, and the deposed king, Christian II, whose fortunes were tied to the papal power in Rome.

Vincens Lunge, a prominent Danish nobleman with three doctorates (philosophy, Roman law and canon law), went to Norway in 1523 on an errand for Frederik I. While there, he married Inger's daughter. Shortly afterwards, Inger's husband died and the young nobleman took over the management of her estates and remained permanently in Norway.

Lunge's brilliant mind understood the use of power and soon convinced western and northern Norway to recognize Frederik's claim to rule. It wasn't long before large additional areas of land fell under Inger's control. Some of these lands were confiscated from the church, which was the largest landowner in Norway. This brought Inger into conflict with Archbiship Olaf Engelbriktson of Trondheim. When necessary, the Archbishop also raised armies to enforce the church's claims. Soon there was open war between them for reasons of real estate and religion. Lunge was also rewarded by King Frederik for his loyalty by giving him a monastery in Bergen and its 272 outlying farms. This is not the first time that nobility, kings and bishops had been in conflict. In these struggles, the masses of people were usually ignored, but they paid for the conflicts with their property and blood.

Christian II, the Danish king in exile, landed an army in Oslo to lay seige to Akerhus Castle and regain his kingdom. Another of Inger's sons-in-law, Nils Lykke, was sent by Frederik with a fleet to rescue the city. Christian again went into exile, but finally surrendered at Oslo and was imprisoned by Frederick I in Denmark and spent the rest of his life in a Danish prison.

The struggle between the Archbishop and Lady Inger was ultimately a disaster for both of them. There were instances where they joined forces, but not for long. Lunge and Lykke died treacherously at the Archbishop's direction. When the new Danish king, Christian III, declared "Lutheranism" to be the official church of Denmark and Norway in 1536, Engelbriktson fled Norway. As he left, he plundered Inger's home at Austraat of much of its treasures.

Inger obtained new Danish husbands for her bereaved daughters, but of lower status in nobility. In 1555, at the age of 80, she suffered shipwreck on a trip to Bergen and was drowned. She has been called "the last representative of Norway's old nobility" and combined an unusual mixture of talent, ambition and thirst for power.

All the contestants in this power struggle were jealous for Norwegian independence and were sincere in what they believed was right both towards God and country. But the tide of events was on the side of Inger and her Danish sons-in-law.

NORWEGIAN STORIES: ANCIENT AND MEDIEVAL

Ever since Emperor Contantine the Great (305-337) decided to combine the Roman Empire with the kingdom of God, the church has had the "protection" of the Caesar's sword. It has also paid the price of becoming the "pawn" of the world's great power brokers. Just as the original conversion of Norway to Christianity was accompanied by violence, so also was its Reformation.

Lady Inger played no small part in these events which have had such a major influence on latter-day Norwegians. One of the mysteries of the human story is that despite the exploitations of Jesus' gospel, both by friends and foes, its influence continues to keep faith and love alive in the most difficult times.

CHAPTER 18

'Prillar-Guri:' The Country Girl Who Saved Norway

PERHAPS YOU HAVE SEEN a picture of a Norwegian girl playing a long horn called a "lur." If so, it was likely meant to be "Prillar-Guri." It's a story that inspires courage and patriotism. The year was 1612. There was war between the joint kingdom of Denmark-Norway and Sweden. In those days, there were often disputes between the Scandinavian powers that led to military conflicts.

The political decisions for the joint kingdom were made in Copenhagen. King Christian IV was the leader of a kingdom joined by the "Union of Kalmar" in 1397, when Margaret I was queen. In this war, the Swedish King had recruited mercenaries from Holland and Scotland to come to his aid.

It has happened only a few times in history that the "savior" of a nation has been a woman, and hardly ever a girl of 17. Guri was an exception. She played a key role in defending the land. For over 350 years, the story of "Prillar-Guri" had been told, but no book could be found on it. In 1968, Arthur Stavig went to Norway to look for the complete story. After a painstaking search, he discovered it was being serialized in the *Romsdal Budstikke*, a daily newspaper. He took the story back to America and together with Marvel Arseth DeSordi translated it into English. Now the whole world can read about this heroine of old Norway.

Guri was an orphan and had been reared by foster parents in Romsdalen, near Molde. She had been a sickly girl and for this reason was taken to an old stave church up in the File Mountains (Filefjell) for prayers of healing. St. Thomas Church was the place for pilgrims to visit on Annunciation Day (March 25). Many of them left their crutches behind as they journeyed home. Whether it was the prayers, the long hike in the mountain air or a combination of both, we do not know, but Guri became radiantly healthy. She was getting ready for her wedding to Kjell, just as soon as he returned from the war. Little did they suspect that their lives would be tragically changed by an event already in progress of which they were innocent. Invading mercenaries would pass directly through their valley.

The Scots might have travelled through to Sweden with little incident, as did the Dutch through Trondheim, if their leader, Col. George Sinclair, had not decided on a campaign of terror to conquer Norway first. Sinclair was a soldier with a charisma for leadership but whose ambition would not hesitate to employ the vilest treachery. His army, with two notable exceptions, was a band of cut-throats, recruited from the lowest dregs of society in western Europe. Their arrival on August 10 began a 16-day reign of terror which has not been forgotten. Every farm building was burned to the ground, children and old people murdered and maidens were ravished. They looted and feasted on whatever food and liquor they could find. To make it even more frightful, Sinclair had a huge bloodhound named "Ralf" that was able to sniff out people and farms at a great distance.

Because of the war with Sweden, there were only old men with crude weapons to defend the valley which led to Gudbrandsdal, Kjell's home. Beyond that lay the unguarded heartland of central Norway. It was Guri, the seter girl, who carried the warning to the unsuspecting farmlands. She travelled through streams and underbrush, hiding from Sinclair and his dog. He had seen her and had resolved to make her his prize of war. She travelled without regard to pain and danger of the wild animals in the mountains. With every breath, she prayed, "Lord Jesus, lead me to warn the people and to save Kjell's family from this terrible enemy". When she arrived at the end of her journey, she didn't look much like a bride. But the people had been warned and now worked feverishly to build an ambush at a narrow pass near Kringen, upstream from Lesje and Dovre.

In the strangest of happenings, Mary Sinclair was also hurrying through the mountains, trying to stop her husband. Carrying her new born son, she wept bitter tears at her husband's deeds.

An avalanche of rocks was constructed to greet the invaders. Just beyond a bend on a narrow pass, a barricade was built. Across the river in plain sight of the enemy stood Guri. She was dressed in her bridal clothes, her wedding with Kjell having just been completed, as he had unexpectedly returned from the war. Guri played her lur as a signal to the defenders that the hated enemy was approaching.

A musket shot from the bushes mortally wounded Sinclair. Then the rocks began to roll. Almost all of the 800 invaders perished. Of the survivors, only 16 escaped massacre by the angry farmers.

The victory for Norway brought a tragic end to Guri's dreams. In the aftermath of the mellee, Kjell tried to save Sinclair's son from harm. The child's mother, overcome with grief and fearing for her son, misunderstood Kjell's intentions and stabbed him to death. Guri's marriage lasted only hours, but she is remembered for what took place at Kringen that day, Aug. 26, 1612. "Prillar-Guri" will live forever as a national hero in Norway's long struggle for freedom.

CHAPTER 19

Norwegian Folk
Tales — Retold

"IF NORWAY WERE TO SHOW THE WORLD a single work of art which would most truly express the Norwegian character, perhaps the best choice would be the folk tales," wrote Pat Shaw Iverson, a recognized writer of Norwegian stories.

Two names are especially remembered in the collecting of these tales. Peter Christian Asbjornsen was born in Oslo in 1812. As a child, he heard these stories ("eventyr") from people who worked in his father's glazier shop. They came from all parts of Norway to learn how to set glass. On their Sunday hikes through fields and forest, they would take young Peter along and excite his imagination with their stories.

In 1826, Asbjornsen met Jorgen Moe, a farm boy from Ringerike in eastern Norway at Norderhov School. They used every spare moment to hunt, fish, hike and dream of becoming poets.

They got the idea of collecting Norwegian folk stories by reading Grimm's fairy tales from Germany. Their first volume was published in 1845. Jacob Grimm had high praise for their work, saying that the Norwegian folk tales had a freshness and fulness which "surpass nearly all others." They went up and down the valleys listening to stories, especially in Gudbrandsdal and Telemark.

In 1879, an illustrated edition was published with hand drawn pictures by Erik Werenskiold of Kongsvinger. He had studied art both in Oslo and Munich. Later Theodore Kittelson of Kragero joined him as an illustrator. Fortunately, this book, entitled *Norwegian Folk Tales*, was re-published in 1982.

In these stories, kings are usually pictured as going around in slippers and smoking long pipes. The clergy, too, were caricatured as being out of touch with the facts of life.

One of my favorite folk tales is called "The Old Woman Against the Stream." These words, "Kjerringa mot strommen," have become a common expression for a stubborn woman. She was so contrary that while arguing with her husband about how to harvest the crop, he drowned her in the river. When she disappeared, he began to think it a pity that she hadn't been given a Christian burial. But alas, her body was nowhere to be found. With the help of friends, he searched everywhere downstream. She had totally disappeared! Then the truth dawned on him. He said, "This old woman of mine had a mind of her own. She was so contrary while she was alive that can't very well be otherwise now. We'll have to start searching upstream." And sure enough, they found that she had floated against the stream and had come to rest above the waterfall! This is genuine Norse humor and everyone would laugh until their insides ached.

As a boy, I enjoyed reading the "Reynard the Fox" stories. I was surprised to find them also in the Asbjornsen-Moe collection. There are a number of troll stories too, including "Billy Goat Gruff."

Many of these tales are common to several European countries and were brought into Norway during the Middle Ages by bards, or storytellers. In the age before television, the storytellers were warmly welcomed into people's homes. Just imagine these stories being told by flickering candlelight in a kitchen with low ceilings during the long winter night or in front of the fireplace. Iverson stated: "The old women usually kept to deep, mystic or eerie themes, while the men related humorous, sometimes bawdy stories."

Another tale that I find amusing is about "The Parson and the Sexton." The parson was an arrogant fellow who would demand the whole road whenever he drove his horse and buggy. His bluff was called one day when he met a man who turned out to be the king. He was ordered to appear in court the next day and be prepared to answer three questions. His job and life depended on the answers.

Not being so good at quizzes, he sent the sexton (a lay assistant) in his place dressed in clergy clothes. The sexton gave very clever answers which satisfied the king. Finally, the king said: "Since you are so wise on all counts, tell me what I'm thinking now!" He replied, "Oh, I suppose you're thinking that it is the parson who's standing here before you. But I'm sorry to say that you're wrong, for it's the sexton." "Aha! Then go home with you, and you be the parson and let him be the sexton," said the king. And so it was.

NORWEGIAN STORIES: ANCIENT AND MEDIEVAL

Are folk stories and fairy tales fit subjects for adult minds? Aren't they meant to tease the imaginations of children? I must admit to losing much of my childhood appreciation for this kind of literature during my years of professional study. But I've changed. I like the inscription written in a well worn book of fairy tales by Hans Christian Andersen in our home. It reads: "Nothing can be truer than fairy wisdom. It is as true as sunbeams." I think, however, that only children and adults who have some of a child's nature in them will be apt to agree.

The Violinist, a woodcarving.

CHAPTER 20

The Tales
Of Askeladden

FOLK TALES TELL A GREAT DEAL about a nation. Every country has its special stories which describe the humor, wit and wisdom by which they have survived. Two Norwegian writers made a great effort to collect the stories of their people before the outside world made its modernizing impact on them. Peter Christian Asbjorsen and Jorgen Moe became friends when they were school boys. They loved to hunt, fish, hike and dream of becoming poets.

Influenced by Grimm's fairy tales from Germany, they travelled up and down the valleys of Norway during the 1840s, especially in Gudbrandsdal and Telemark, listening to the stories which had been told for generations. The people never tired of telling or hearing them again and again. It was their main entertainment during the long dark nights of winter.

Among the favorite stories were those of Askeladden, "the Ash Boy." He was the "Cinderella" of the boy's world. His main job was tending the fire and raking the ashes in the fireplace. His two older brothers scorned him because of his simple honesty. They were "bigshots" in their own eyes. Even his mother merely tolerated him. In the stories, of course, Askeladden always comes out on top, much to the chagrin of everyone except the listeners.

Once there was a king whose daughter was an atrocious liar. He offered any man who could get her to say, "You're a liar," that he'd get half the kingdom and the princess for a wife. When the older brothers failed, Askeladden ventured forth to the castle and managed to always tell a taller tale than the princess. He won the prize.

In another story, Askeladden matched wits and courage with a big, burly Troll in the forest. The older brothers had been sent into the forest to chop wood. As soon as the chips started to fly, the Troll would say, "If you're chopping in my forest, I'm going to kill you!" They threw away

51

their axes and ran for dear life until they got home. Askeladden had never been away from home before, but he confidently set out for the forest. When confronted with the Troll, he took some cheese from his knapsack and squeezed it until whey ran out of it and said, "If you don't hold your tongue, I'll squeeze you the way I'm squeezing water out of this white stone." With that, the Troll became cooperative and invited the boy to his home where he challenged him to an eating contest. Fortunately for Askeladden, Trolls are a bit dim witted and have weak eyes. The Ash Boy kept putting the food into his knapsack hanging over his stomach and slit it when full. When the Troll could eat no more, Askeladden advised him to slit his stomach, as he had done to his knapsack. The Troll did so and Askeladden marched home with all the silver and gold found in the mountain.

In another story, the king offered his daughter and half of the kingdom to anyone who could build a ship that could go as fast on land as on sea. The proclamation was read in all the churches of the land. Askeladden had managed to get away from the ashes and be at the service that day. His older brothers set out for the prize and on the way met a bent and wizened old man. When he asked what they were doing, they lied and everything turned out badly.

When Askeladden's turn came, his honesty and wits always carried him through to success, even when the king tried to renig on the deal. He didn't like the Ash Boy's dirty clothes. Finally, he grudgingly gave Askeladden both princess and kingdom.

People never tire of these morality stories where the simple triumph over the wise, the weak over the strong and where honesty pays handsome dividends. The people who lived in the valleys of Norway were mostly poor and these stories kept hope alive even when they had little else than "hope."

CHAPTER 21

The Historic
Tingvoll Church

"REMOVE NOT THE ANCIENT landmarks," warned the prophets of Israel. The Tingvoll Church in Nordmore, western Norway, is a classic example of an old site which continues to have meaning in the 20th century.

The Tingvoll Church lies along the route between Molde and Trondheim. We visited there in 1984. A "Ting" or "Thing" was the assembly of free farmers and the "voll" is a grassy meadow. The farmers met there as the local legislative body. Tingvoll was in use for such meetings in the Viking days, even before Christianity came to Norway. It was the custom to build a church on important Viking sites to show the victory of Christ over the Norse gods. If you visit the stave church in Bergen, you'll see a granite cross atop an old Viking mound.

Built in the late 12th century, about 800 years ago, the Tingvoll Church was restored in 1929 by Architect Sivert Glaerum from Surnadal, my ancestral community. Constructed like a fortress, the walls are 40 inches thick and have passages built into them. Churches, like castles, were used both for worship and defense. It is believed that the site has Christian connections since the days of King Olaf Tryggvason who died in 1000.

The furnishings are what especially intrigued me. It contains a Bible from 1589 and candlesticks from 1624. The pews date to 1613. The baptismal font was done by artists from Nuremberg, Germany, and dates somewhere between 1400 and 1600. The chalice is pre-Reformation. The crucifix dates to 1664. On the west wall at the front of the nave is the traditional ship which hangs in Scandiavian churches. This one is a model of a 17th century war frigate, draped with Norwegian flags. Carvings of the four evangelists (Matthew, Mark, Luke and John) are mounted on the pulpit and were believed to have been made by a pupil of El Greco. High above the ornately carved altar are statues of Christ on the cross with his sorrowing mother and a disciple standing beneath.

Noticeable to an American visitor is the absence of windows in these old churches and those that you see are small and high, as you'd expect on a defense installation.

Outside the white stucco covered stone building is the typical country cemetery. On one tombstone from the 1300s is the inscription, "Here lies Ingeborg who married Anders. Pray to God for her soul." On top of the steeple is the weather vane, typical of Norwegian churches.

There is much more to the Tingvoll Church than fancy art work from bygone days. The Nordmore area is famous for its music. It has its own history of folk melodies which have a beauty recognized all over Norway. Edvard Braein (1887-1957), an organist and composer, collected most of the living folk music from the Nordmore area before Norway became bombarded with American and British music. (Now the tendency is to make everyone's music alike by imitating whoever happens to be the current star.) Almost 4000 of his collected melodies were recently discovered in an attic. It has been described as a "cultural bomb in Norway."

An unusual opportunity for people of the Midwest USA was held in the summer of 1986 when three musicians from Nordmore did a Minnesota-North Dakota concert tour. Members of the group included soloist Dordi Bergheim. She requested this tour so she could sing "to her dear relatives in North Dakota." Ola Braein, son of Edvard Braein, is a classical harmonica player. He studied under Sigmund Groven who has performed for the Norsk Høstfest. Tor Strand, one of Norway's young leading organists, is the organist in the Tingvoll Church. Most of the musical arrangements have been done by Henning Sommerro, regarded as one of Norway's leading young composers. This music of Nordmore is to Norway what the Negro spirituals are to America. It's language of the soul.

The mountainous interior of Norway was separated from the European centers of influence so that many of its traditions have continued to this present day. The Tingvoll Church is one of the ancient landmarks of Norway that still stands.

CHAPTER 22

'Gamle Norge —
Old Norway'

"**K**AN DU GLEMME GAMLE NORGE?" ("Can you forget old Norway?") This song is still sung by the children of immigrants who have never seen the shores of that far north land. But what was "old Norway" like? Jon Leirfall, from Stjordalen in the Trondheim area, has written an excellent book entitled *Old Times in Norway*. It's one of the most helpful books I've read to understand the Norway which shaped the lives of the immigrant period (1825-1925).

Leirfall, born in 1899, is famous in Norway both as a writer and a politician. He was a prominent leader in the Farmer's Party (Bondepartiet) and was a member of the Parliament from 1945 to 1969. He is a "grass roots" historian with a good sense of humor. He is also an honorary citizen of Minneapolis. Leirfall attended the 1986 Norsk Høstfest and was introduced as a relative of Myron Floren. I found him to be a delightful gentleman.

According to Leirfall, the new Norway began to emerge about 1840, although it took several generations before the change was complete. I suspect that traces of "old Norway" are as likely to be found in some parts of America as in Norway today. Reading his book helped me to understand my own past. There are some things that I had supposed were the peculiarities of the immigrants which really are rooted in a thousand or more years of culture. It was only in America that they stood out as "different."

Leirfall explains the terminology needed to understand life in the old country. Such terms as "bygd" (rural community), "gaard" (farm), "grend" (neighborhood), "Opphavsgaard" (the original farm site) and "smaabruk" (cotter's farm) are explained with examples. He tells what it was like to be a child growing up in those days when education, though limited, was highly honored, making the Norwegian immigrants some of the most literate newcomers to America. That's why they rose quickly to positions of leadership, especially in politics.

NORWEGIAN STORIES: ANCIENT AND MEDIEVAL

In the age before instant communications, evenings were spent around the fireplace telling and re-telling the stories that were part of the community. The parafin lamp and the kitchen stove greatly altered this pattern.

I enjoyed his description of the cotter's life. These were the small farmers on the edge of the main farm. Since the big farm went by law to the oldest son (for which he was bound to care for his parents as long as they lived), younger sons had to move out. Many of them cleared patches of ground on the mountain sides and eked out a living by their tiny cottages. The cotter also had to work for the "bønde" (the boss farmer) to pay rent. When the emigration to northern Norway and America took place, thousands of these cottages became vacant and farm workers became scarce.

It was not long before letters from America arrived about the wonders of the New World with its opportunities and freedom. When some of the successful emigrants began to return, usually at Christmas time, they were honored almost as royalty. All their past sins and foolishness for leaving Norway were forgiven.

During the 19th century, after Norway came under the rule of the Swedish king, a spirit of nationalism arose. The constitution of 1814 inspired the drive to have a completely free nation to choose its own destiny. With the overload of population going mostly to America (800,000 out of a population of 1,700,000 in 1865), poverty decreased and the rights of the common man were asserted. The cotters (just the men) were given the right to vote in 1884 and universal manhood suffrage was granted in 1897. Norway was second only to Finland in giving women the right to vote.

During the Danish period (1380-1814) when Norway was ruled from Copenhagen, the written language took on a great deal of Danish spelling. During the Swedish Period (1814-1905), Norwegians started to return to the "Old Norse." For example, "Hagen" was restored to "Haakon," especially in respect to their new king, Haakon VII (1905-1958). "Dahl" (valley) returned to "dal." My maternal grandmother's name was Beret. I wondered why her mother and grandmother, besides two sisters had this name. Leirfall explains that custom dictated the names of both sons and daughters. My mother's name Anne, as well as Jorun, has occurred for many generations in our family. The name Anne (pronounced "Anneh") is carried through to one of our granddaughters. That's a good Norwegian custom.

The big event of the community was a wedding. In the old days, the party could last for a whole week. Among my Halling ancestors, this could be a frightning time. The "kniv-Hallings" wore knives and fighting often erupted when too much liquor was served at these drawn out celebrations. In anticipation of this, many wives packed their husband's burial clothes when they went to a "bryllup" (wedding). The morning after the ceremony, they were all served "Rommegrot" (cream porridge) for breakfast. This continues to be a delicacy among many children of immigrants.

The old ways have passed. And it's a good thing, too, because they were filled with unnecessary taboos and fears. Infant mortality was high, so was death through childbirth. Medical understanding was extremely limited. Still, those days continue to beckon with nostalgia and we continue to sing, "Kan du glemme gamle Norge?" Leirfall helps us not to forget.

*Anne Marie
Gaylor
in her
Bunad.*

PART II

Norwegian Stories: Immigration Period

CHAPTER 23

Hans Nielsen Hauge —
Norway's Greatest Folk Hero

NOBODY HAS HAD SO GREAT an influence on the people of Norway in modern times as Hans Nielsen Hauge. This influence was carried to the New World by over 800,000 immigrants.

Who was Hauge and why was he so important? He was born on April 3, 1771, about 50 miles southeast of Oslo. The "Hauge Gaard" (farm) was small and could afford Hans only a minimal education. Yet he learned the three "R's" well and was good at carpentry and blacksmithing. He even invented his own tools and he had a good head for business.

Despite these practical skills, his foremost interest was religion. Hans was reared in a pious home with daily Bible reading, prayers and where the catechism was studied together with Luther's sermons. Hans went with his parents to Bible studies led by laymen. One question bothered him: "What does God require of me?" So he applied himself to studying Scripture and theology at home. Though everything was clear in his head, his heart was full of uncertainty. One day when he was 25, while singing a hymn behind a plow, he felt he was being lifted to heaven. This changed his life and Hans was persuaded that God had called him to be a "preacher."

Hauge travelled over 10,000 miles to almost every part of Norway in all kinds of weather. The common people responded to him with enthusiasm. But there was a law which forbade unauthorized persons from preaching. The authorities were afraid that he might lead a peasant revolt. Between 1796 and 1804, he was arrested 10 times and accused of all kinds of crimes, including murder and witchcraft.

The authorities in Copenhagen decided that Hauge would have to be punished. He was taken to Akershus Castle and locked in a soggy dungeon for several years. Later he was put into a small room with a barred window in a two-story house for 10 years. Today, visitors can see this house in Bygdøy Park, chains and all.

Hauge had proven business skills and had built paper mills, grist mills, printing houses and salt factories. These supported his evangelistic work which was carried out through many friends. During a war with England in 1809, he was released from jail to build more salt factories, as Norway's supplies were cut off.

Though opposed by the State Church, Hauge held no bitterness. One of his sons became a pastor in the State Church in Skien. His health broke under the strain of prison and he was released at Christmas 1814 upon paying a heavy fine. Since he could travel no more, a constant stream of visitors came to him until he died 10 years later.

Today, Hauge is honored throughout Norway and especially in the churches where he was once forbidden to speak. In America, there was a "Hauge Synod" among Norwegian Lutherans. Though he emphasized repentance and personal faith, yet he also is recognized in Norway today as a "folk leader" among the common people. He could never forget that he was the son of a farmer. I know the feeling.

CHAPTER 24

The Haugeans
At Eidsvoll

NO POPULAR MOVEMENT affected Norway more than the one that grew out of the work of Hans Nielsen Hauge (1771-1824). "Haugeanism" played a major role in the tide of events which led to the constitution written at Eidsvoll on May 17 ("Syttende Mai"), 1814. Like most people in Norway, the followers of Hauge were mostly farmers and operators of small businesses. In 1700, the population of Norway was only 500,000, of whom 92% lived on farms. By 1800, the population had grown to almost 900,000 of whom 87% were farmers.

Norway and Sweden were the only two European countries where the common people retained freedom during the Middle Ages. These farmers, called "bønde," were the backbone of the country even before the days of St. Olaf. Between 1770 and 1814, an aristrocracy developed among these farmers, while a poorer class of agricultural laborers ("husmaend" or "crofters") lived in small cottages ("hytter") along the edge of the main farms. By 1807, there were 48,500 such poorer farmers. Despite their dependent financial status, however, they did not lose their rights as free people.

While Haugeanism was essentially a religious movement, emphasizing repentance and personal faith, it also had its political and social significance. In the earlier years of Danish rule (1380-1814), Danes and Germans held the majority of high positions in government. However, by 1814, more Norwegians held official positions in Denmark than Danes did in Norway.

The early 1800s were years of ferment. Napoleon set out to conquer the continent. When Denmark reluctantly entered the war on the Emperor's side, England's Lord Nelson wasted no time in destroying the Danish navy and merchant marine. In 1814, England forced the Danish king to cede Norway to the King of Sweden. This was a signal to the Norwegians to determine their own destiny. Prince Kristian Fredrik of

Denmark almost persuaded the Norwegians to declare their independence and to elect him king. Georg Sverdrup, however, advised him that he had no right to the throne unless the Norwegian people chose him. So the prince invited 21 of Norway's outstanding men to meet at Eidsvoll on Feb. 16, 1814, to formulate a plan of action.

A day of prayer was held throughout the land and delegates were elected from all the parishes. They met at Eidsvoll, 40 miles north of Oslo. Three men from each district were chosen for the assembly, of whom one had to be a farmer. Beginning on Easter Sunday, April 10, the 120 men concluded their work and signed the new constitution on May 17. Several prominent Haugeans were among them.

The farmers were not as well educated as the aristocracy, but the Haugeans had their champions, including Sverdrup. Two groups emerged. The Independence Party, with about 80 members, wanted complete independence. The "Unionists," with about 30 members, favored a union with Sweden in which the Norwegian constitution would be honored. The farmers wanted independence, perhaps in part because of lingering loyalty to the Danish king, but the "Unionists" prevailed. They knew that Norway would be invaded by battle-toughened Swedish soldiers and that their coasts would be blockaded by the British navy. Representatives from Russia and Prussia warned the Norwegians against claiming independence. Austria concurred in this decision.

The new constitution looked back to the ancient laws before Norway was united by King Harald Harfagre in 872. It was an appeal for the freedom of the common people who operated small farms. "Civil liberties" were incorporated into the constitution, which also was patterned in some respects after the new American and French documents. The Norwegians accepted Karl Johan as their new king. He, in turned, agreed to respect their constitution.

The aristocrats in Christiania (Oslo), the new capital, claimed special privileges. They passed a law to draft only rural men for the army, but the officers were to come from the upper classes. Local revolts took place but these were swiftly put down by the central government. By 1833, the farmers started to organize and gained 45 seats in the Storting (Parliament). New leadership emerged as they gained control of the government.

Among the able Haugeans involved in this agrarian movement was John Gabriel Ueland. It is not by accident that another member of that family, Lars Ueland, later sponsored the "initiative and referendum" in North Dakota, the first of its kind in the nation. John Ueland spent 37 years (1833-1870) in the Storting. He often said that "the Norwegian people's two most precious pearls are their religion and their constitution." Georg Sverdrup entered the Storting in 1851 and also championed the cause of freedom.

The Haugeans were concerned about "true religion." To them, this meant that they acted out their faith in the political and social realms. This influence followed the immigrants to America where they energetically became social reformers and political activists.

The "aristocrats," for the most part, did not migrate to the New World. They stayed in Norway to look after their investments. And while "new aristocracies" have developed among the "new rich" in America, some of the energy that produced their success can be traced to that movement started by Hans Nielsen Hauge, the simple lay preacher, who tirelessly walked the breadth and length of the land to call people to renewal of faith.

Hans Nielsen Hauge.

CHAPTER 25

Herman Wedel Jarlsberg — A Statesman To Be Remembered

"**J**ARLSBERG" IS THE NAME OF A CHEESE imported from Norway. It's also the name of the largest farm in Norway, located 100 miles southwest of Oslo, with 30,000 acres under cultivation. The farm house is a castle built in 1701.

In the old days, Norway was ruled mainly by nobles who elected the kings at the "Thing" assemblies. Power struggles between the kings and the nobles were common. After the Black Death of 1349, the nobles and their extensive land holdings were almost wiped out. Then came the Danish period (1397-1814) when Norway was ruled from Copenhagen. The Danish kings would secure the services of German families of noble background to administer Norway for them. This is also how the Preus family came to Norway from Germany, according to Prof. Kris Skrondal.

One of these German nobles was Peter Schumacher, known as Count Griffenfeld. When he fell from royal favor, he spent the rest of his life in prison on Munkholmen in Trondheim harbor. His vast land holdings ended up in the hands of another German family. It was sold to a baron, Field Marshall General Wilhelm von Wedel. He was from Oldenburg in northwest Germany, also the origin of the royal family of Denmark-Norway from 1448-1863. Von Wedel commanded Norway's military forces. The name given to the farm was "Jarlsberg," which means the "Jarl's hill." A "jarl" (an earl), was a rank of nobility next to royalty. It reminds me of a game we played as children called "King of the Hill."

Twelve generations of Wedel Jarlsbergs have lived on this farm. Those of us from peasant stock may not always feel too charitable towards aristocratic families. However, the Wedel Jarlsbergs are an example of a noble line that has rendered invaluable service that was beyond the capability of peasants.

One of the most famous of these was Herman Wedel Jarlsberg (1779-1840). He played a major role in writing the constitution of 1814

65

which Norwegians love to celebrate every May 17. It was his leadership which guided the writing of Norway's civil rights and persuaded the Swedish king, Karl Johan, to honor it. He favored Norway electing the king of Sweden to be its new royalty after England forced out the Danes. In 1836, he became the "Statholder" (representative) in Oslo for the Swedish king.

Herman Wedel Jarlsberg married the only daughter of Peder Anker from Bogstad near Oslo and inherited his estate of 5,500,000 acres of land, plus saw mills, iron works and other industries. Another wealthy Norwegian, Carsten Anker, opened his house at Eidsvoll for the constitutional assembly meetings. The good thing that has to be said about these very rich people is that they championed the cause of democracy while staying on good terms with royalty. Afterall, kings have no money except what they collect in taxes, and the Ankers and Wedel Jarlsbergs were highly successful businessmen. So the next time you pass a cheese counter and read "Jarlsberg," remember that it is a name which Norwegians honor.

CHAPTER 26

'Syttende Mai' —
Norway's Constitution Day

MAY 17 - "SYTTENDE MAI" - is Norway's happiest holiday. How did it start and what does it mean? On that day in 1814, 112 men signed a new constitution for Norway. They had been elected from the Lutheran state church parishes. They had travelled by foot, skis, horseback and wagons from every part of Norway except the far northern parts, Nordland and Finnmark. Travel was not possible from those wintry areas. The delegates met at Eidsvoll in the home of Carsten Anker, a wealthy merchant. Eidsvoll is about 40 miles north of Oslo.

The constitutional assembly met for worship on Easter Sunday. It consisted of 47 officials, 37 farmers, 16 town representatives and 12 from the military. It was called by Christian Frederick, the ruling representative of the Danish king. The purpose of the assembly was to save Norway from an uncertain future. The majority of the delegates favored declaring Norway an independent monarchy with the Prince Christian Frederick as the new monarch. He was not unwilling.

It was an age of revolutions and a time for redrawing the maps of Europe and the New World. A new nation, the United States of America, had adopted a constitution in 1787 based on freedom and justice for all. The might of Britain had been repulsed. In France too, a once powerful monarchy had been overthrown and a new constitution was adopted in 1791.

An international crisis had started the chain of events rolling. As "punishment" for siding with the French, England and its allies had forced the Danish king to give up claim to Norway at the Treaty of Kiel on Jan. 14, 1814. This ended a joint rule begun in 1380 and which lasted 434 years. The Norwegians had not even been consulted! Ironically, Norway's possessions, Iceland, Greenland the Faroe Islands, were overlooked in the treaty and became Danish colonies by default. Norway was promised to Sweden as compensation for the loss of Finland to Russia in 1809.

NORWEGIAN STORIES: IMMIGRATION PERIOD

The Eidsvoll assembly was a bold stroke for independence. Why couldn't Norway be free? The delegates studied the new American and French constitutions. It was also known that Karl Johan of the Bernadotte family in France, who had become Sweden's new crown prince in 1810, would rather have returned to France as its new king rather than wait for his future in Sweden. He never did learn the Swedish language. The French, however, restored the Bourbon family to power and Karl Johan chose to cash in on his fortune in Sweden with Norway as a bonus.

Brave talk, however, is not enough to secure freedom. The British navy blockaded Norway and cut off its needed food supplies as well as all exports. The economy crumbled. By the end of July, Karl Johan personally took command of his battle hardened troops. They were superior to Norway's "home guard" in numbers, training and equipment. Fighting lasted less than two weeks. The pro-Swedish faction in Norway's Storting (parliament), headed by Herman Wedel Jarlsberg, held sway. They were no less patriotic, but were realists about international politics. During this time, they were also lobbying in London for more favorable terms. Christian Frederick renounced his claim to be king of Norway and returned to his homeland where he became King Christian VIII, 25 years later. On Nov. 4, 1814, the Storting unanimously elected and recognized Karl XIII, the king of Sweden, as Norway's monarch. Norway, however, remained a separate nation from Sweden and was only beholden to the king.

The Norwegians negotiated a favorable agreement with their new king. The constitution was respected, they were not required to supply troops for Sweden's foreign wars, they could elect and run their own Storting and a representative of the king would reside in Oslo.

Four years later, the French-born Crown Prince of Sweden became King Karl XIV Johan. He would liked to have had Nov. 4 celebrated as a holiday in Norway in recognition of his rule. As in so many things proposed by the Swedish kings, the Norwegians were not agreeable. Instead, a group of students led a demonstration on May 17, 1829, a symbol of their determination for full Norwegian freedom. Still hoping to win the Norsemen over, the king good naturedly allowed "Syttende Mai" to be celebrated.

The "Unions Perioden," as the union with Sweden was called, lasted until Oct. 26, 1905, when the Swedish King Oscar II gave up all rights to Norway. He concluded that it was a hopeless task to govern Norway from Sweden. It was also a time of bad economy and heavy emigration to the New World.

"Syttende Mai" has become as much a symbol of freedom to Norwegians as July 4 to Americans. Norsemen are still celebrating May 17 as their Constitution Day, even though independence didn't come for another 91 years. When independence finally came in 1905, they revised and updated the Eidsvoll constitution and declared it to be "Kongeriget Norges Nye Grundlov" (the Kingdom of Norway's New Constitution). The Eidsvoll assembly had done its work well. Long live the constitution and freedom for Norsemen and their neighbors everywhere!

CHAPTER 27

Ole, The Cotter's Son —
A Story Of Courage And Love

THERE ARE MANY COTTER'S SONS who left the Old World for the New. Their departure did not mean a lack of love for parents or native land. They left because they had a desperate dream for a better life.

A "cotter" (husmann) was a share-cropper who had a cottage on the edge of the main farm. It was often on a hillside and had to first be reclaimed by removing rocks. But this was the only way that a young man could have a home. He could not, of course, expect to accumulate savings. Most of his time was spent working for the landowner, called a "bønde." I have seen these hillside huts. They may look pretty, but they are humble shelters.

Hans Anderson Foss wrote a story called "Husmandsgutten" or "The Cotter's Son." It was first serialized by the Decorah-Posten in 1884 and was claimed to be the most read book written by a Norwegian-American.

The story is about Ole Haugen, born in the Sigdal area west of Oslo. (A "haug" is a hill or hillside. This accounts for his last name.) His parents, Torkil and Randi, were cotters on the land of the wealthiest farmer in the valley. The bønde was a hard man, but his wife was known for her kindness.

The custom in those days was that when there was a baptism or confirmation that the request to the pastor had to be accompanied by a gift of money. It was not unlike the Levitical laws of the Old Testament which prescribed sacrifices. Like Joseph and Mary who could give only a poor family's offering when their son was brought to the Temple, Ole's parents also struggled to provide the prescribed gift. The bønde refused to give Torkil a loan for the baptism, so his wife secretly sent some of her own silver coins to them. The bønde's rule was: "The more you give them, the more they want and the less they will work."

Ole amazed everyone at his confirmation with his sincere and quick answers during the catechization. This was a custom where children publicly recited their knowledge of the Bible and their faith. Some people thought that Ole should be a minister and raised money to send him to school. The bønde, however, put a stop to that. To complicate matters more, the bønde's daughter, Marie, was the same age as Ole. They played together as children and became fast friends. To separate them, Ole was sent up to the seter (mountain pasture) early in the spring. There he stayed wth the farm animals until just before snowfall when he returned for school. The bønde was taking no chances. He didn't want his money to fall into a cotter's family.

Despite the attempts to keep them apart, Ole and Marie came to have a deep love for each other. They realized that the only hope they had for a future together was if Ole went to America. So he went. His best friend in the New World was Nils, also from Norway. He had a brilliant head for business, but was a constant failure to say "no" to the bottle. Ole's friendship gave him the new directions that he needed. He later repaid with good business advice.

It was Ole's intention to send money back to his family and then return to Marie. In his first job, west of Chicago, he was cheated out of wages for the whole summer. So he set out on foot to look for work in Wisconsin, as winter approached. On the way, he was mistaken for a bank robber and was arrested. After his innocence was proved, he was released and nearly lost his life in a snow storm north of Madison. He found refuge with an American family who also gave him a job on their farm. During a sudden winter storm, Ole rescued the family's two teenage daughters at great risk to himself. He carried them to their home in a blinding blizzard. The farm dog led him. One of the daughters, Nellie, survived.

The neighbors, of course, began to talk. Ole's brave deed got into the newspapers and was reprinted in Norway. It also said that Ole was going to marry Nellie! This was all the bønde needed to see. He showed it to Marie, but she refused to believe it. Then the bønde intercepted the mail so that there was no correspondence between Ole and his family or with Marie for a year and a half. Money sent home was also stolen by the bønde.

71

Stories like this were not uncommon, but not all of them had happy endings. In this case, the love between Ole and Marie stood the test. With the help of Nils, Ole made a good business investment in Chicago that made it possible to go back to Norway with lots of money in his pocket. The high point in the story is when Ole bought the bønde's farm at an auction. The mail fraud had caught up with the rich farmer and he died a poor man.

The story has more pathos than can be retold here. But stories like this from the Sigdal-Numedal area have been preserved as a reminder to the children of immigrants that courage and love still have their rewards.

CHAPTER 28

Henrik Ibsen —
'Shakespeare Of The North'

A COUPLE OF HOURS TO THE SOUTHWEST of Oslo is Skien, the birthplace of Henrik Ibsen, who has been called the "Shakespeare of the North." Though he left home after confirmation, he is the best remembered of all its sons. A house on the outskirts of the city where he lived is now a museum in his honor and a beautiful motel bears his name.

Ibsen (1828-1906) spent his early years in poverty, but it did not stifle his imagination. When only six, his father suffered financial ruin. After being apprenticed to an apothecary in Grimstad and studying in Oslo, he worked for six years at Ole Bull's National Theatre in Bergen. Only one of his early plays even had modest success. In 1860-1861, he was so depressed by poverty that he could not write at all.

In 1864, Ibsen moved to Italy. Later, he lived for periods of time in Germany. Distance gave better perspective for his plays. In 1866, he published "Brand," the story of a heartless pastor, which made him famous throughout Scandinavia. His greatest early success was "Peer Gynt," based on an actual person who had lived in Gudbrandsdal. Ibsen had travelled through this valley and heard the old timers tell some of the stories about that ner-do-well rapskalion. Most of what is known about him is found in Asbjørnsen's "Fairy Tales."

Writers often do self portraits. Ibsen wrote: "Nobody can put a character on paper without—at any rate in part and at times—sitting as a model for it himself." There was something of both Brand, the rigid preacher, and Peer Gynt, the fantasizing rebel, in Ibsen. His first plays were written to be read and only years later appeared on stage.

Ibsen, however, was much more than an entertainer. He was a protester of social issues. In *Doll's House* and *Ghosts*, he crusaded for women's rights a hundred years before it became a popular cause.

NORWEGIAN STORIES: IMMIGRATION PERIOD

My favorite scene in Ibsen's plays is in the opening act of Peer Gynt. Peer had run off into the mountains with his gun to hunt reindeer when the farm work was busiest, leaving it all to his mother, Aase. He returned with tattered clothes and without gun or game. She scolded him with fury but was soon taken in by his story of riding a big buck across the mountains. She knew it was a lie but begged him to finish the story. Then she realized the truth and said: "That's the tale of Gudbrand Glesne, not of you." No amount of tears or prayers could change him.

After a wasted life, Peer was about to pay the devil his due by being recycled by a "Button Moulder." Only the love of Solveig, the woman whom he had continually spurned, saved him from that fate. Edvard Grieg immortalized the story by putting it to music in the "Peer Gynt Suite." Ibsen relocated to Norway in 1891 for the last 15 years of his life.

As I stood overlooking the mountain range where Peer had taken his reindeer ride, I asked my friend, Knut Løvseth of Trondheim, if Ibsen had ever hiked through the area. He replied: "Oh, no. He was afraid of Trolls." There is more than a story in each of Ibsen's writings. There is understanding of human nature.

CHAPTER 29

Edvard Grieg
And 'Troldhaugen'

WHEN DENMARK'S FREDERICK VI asked Edvard Grieg who had taught him to play the piano, he replied: "I learned from the mountains of Norway." When people think of Norwegian music, Grieg is usually the first name that comes to mind.

Who was this unusual musician that combined romanticism with patriotism? Edvard Grieg (1843-1907) was the great grandson of a Grieg who had come from Scotland to Bergen. On his mother's side, he descended from the well known Hagerup family. They were highly gifted in music. It was Ole Bull, Norway's famous violinist, who urged that young Edvard study at the Leipzig Conservatory in Germany when he was only fifteen. There he received a classical training.

The music of the continent did not suit Edvard's nature. Another Norwegian musician, Rikard Nordraak (1842-1866), persuaded Grieg to listen to the folk tunes of his own country. He wrote: "Listen to the unclothed plaintive melodies that wander, like so many orphans, around the countryside all over Norway. Gather them about you in a circle round the hearth of love and let them tell you their stories." Grieg did and he enchanted the whole world with these melodies.

To feel close to the music of Grieg, you must go to Bergen and visit Troldhaugen. There you can walk through the summer chalet where Edvard and his wife, Nina, spent many summers. It's on a lake overlooking the Hardangerfjord. "Troldhaugen" means "Troll Hill." He built a small hut by the water's edge where he spent many hours alone with the piano and musical scores. The dampness was not good for his health, but he could not give up Troldhaugen.

In Rome, Grieg was highly acclaimed by Franz Liszt. He was compared to Chopin. Whenever you listen to Grieg, you can hear some notes from Norway's folk dances. This does not find favor with some critics of the classical tradition. One of his favorite authors was Hans

Christian Andersen. He wrote the music to Andersen's "Jeg elsker dig" ("I Love Thee"), a favorite to this day.

Grieg had a definite purpose with his music: "My aim is what Ibsen expresses in his drama, namely to build homes for the people, in which they can be happy and contented." Queen Victoria told him: "I am a great admirer of your compositions."

Grieg has done for Norway what Sibelius did for Finland. He took the sounds of of nature and has put them to music so that the whole world can hear them. In 1949, when the Concordia College Concert Choir of Moorhead, Minnesota, was on tour to Bergen, Director Paul J. Christiansen took off his shoes before entering the house at Troldhaugen. This was his way of paying tribute to one of Norway's greatest.

The movie, "The Song of Norway," tells the story of Grieg. But best of all, listen to his music and, if possible, visit Troldhaugen. The foliage on the pathway to the house is a lush green. Down by the lakeside, you can see their burial crypt, imbedded into the side of a rock. He was a romantic to the end. And if you listen carefully, you can hear still hear the piano playing the tunes of the waterfalls and mountain winds.

Grieg's composing hut.

CHAPTER 30

The Icebreaker
'Fram'

ACROSS THE ROAD FROM the farm where I grew up in Richland County, North Dakota, there is a township called Nanson. We farmed some of that land. Later, I doscovered that it was named after a famous Norwegian, Fridtjof Nansen ("-sen" endings were often changed to "-son" in America). Nansen became world famous for Arctic explorations and for the icebreaker which he designed. On my first visit to Norway, I saw the ship now on permanent display near the Kon-Tiki Museum at Bygdøy Park in Oslo.

When Nansen went to London in 1892 to present his plans for Arctic exploration to the Royal Geographical Society, his plan was deemed doomed to disaster. But Nansen was a true scientist with a Nordic understanding of the polar regions. His ship was 128 feet long and 36 feet at its widest. The layers of planking were between 24 and 28 inches thick, with the spaces between filled with pitch to make it watertight. The bottom was almost flat. The height of the mainmast was 80 feet and the crow's nest was 102 feet above the waterline. It had a three cylinder engine capable of seven knots in calm water. The ship was named the "Fram," which means "Forward," a fit description of Nansen's spirit.

Nansen said good-byes to his wife and daughter on June 23, 1893, and sailed out of the Oslo harbor around Norway's west coast. The commander was Otto Sverdrup from a well known Norwegian family who was also a scientist. There was a crew of 12. Wherever they stopped, they were given farewell parties. On July 21, they left the coast of Norway. Stopping at islands, they hunted for meat. By mid-August, they encountered storms and by October 1 they were sitting on ice. Polar bears visited them several times. One came on board and killed some of the dogs.

During the winter, there was nothing to do but wait until spring. The snow storms were fierce, long and cold, down to minus 56 degrees.

77

Despite their situation, they celebrated Christmas with a gourmet dinner, including fish pudding and cloudberries. The 17th of May (Constitution Day) was greeted with outbursts of patriotism. The Fram sailed all summer and went 2000 miles east of Norway on the north coast of Siberia before it began its return trek. On March 14, 1895, Nansen and Lt. Frederick Johansen left the Fram by dog sled for the polar cap. On April 7, 1895, they stopped, 226 miles from their goal, but 200 miles closer than anyone had ever been. They could go no further. After a perilous journey by sled and kayak, Nansen returned to Norway in mid August. All his dogs had had to be killed. A few days later, Sverdrup arrived with the Fram. The expedition was hailed as a great scientific success. Oxford and Cambridge gave honorary degrees to Nansen, then 34 years old.

Nansen did not return to the Arctic, but served his country well through teaching and statecraft. He had become the most famous man in all Norway. What were his future conquests? That remains for another story. But if you go to Oslo, see the Fram for yourself. It still looks like a grand ship.

CHAPTER 31

Immigrants From
Voss To America

I S THERE ANY PLACE IN NORWAY that did not pour out its people to come to America? Not since the Black Death of 1349 did Norway lose so many of its people as in the emigrations of the 19th century. Only Ireland contributed a larger percent of its population to the New World.

The city of Voss is one of the beauty spots in Norway's "Westlands." Its scenery is captivating and people delightful. The clean shops, the lovely Vangskyrkja (the church) and the landscape exposure to the south make it an ideal place to vacation. The church was built in 1277. Before 1840, there were less than three miles of good roads in the entire district. Not until 1883, when the railroad from Bergen was built, did Voss get a solid connection with the outside world, shortening the travel time between those two points from one week to four hours. Today there is excellent rail and highway travel from Oslo as well.

While "Vossings" have settled in all parts of America, the two largest concentrations have been Koshkonong, near Madison, Wisconsin, and Chicago, a city of only 4000 people when the first Vossings arrived in 1836. (See Odd S. Lovoll's book *A Century of Urban Life: The Norwegians in Chicago Before 1930* — 1988.) I became acquainted with many of them when living in the "Windy City." The first Norwegian club in America was organized in 1848 by Vossings in Chicago who promoted correspondence with Norway.

Two people for whom Voss is especially dear, Jonas and Mabel Wold of Minot, North Dakota, have shared with me a book telling of its emigration, entitled *Gammalt Fra Voss*, (*Old Times from Voss*), written in both Norwegian and English.

Voss offered only a meager living from the soil for its people until the 1930s. When the population started to increase greatly during the middle 18th century, people broke up more land for farming. Most of these were "crofters," or "cotters" who lived on small plots on the edge of the main farms of the valleys.

NORWEGIAN STORIES: IMMIGRATION PERIOD

Despite its remoteness, Voss was known for having a high level of industry and ingenuity. Ivar Aasen (1813-1896), whose statue stands on the campus of Concordia College in Moorhead, Minnesota, and one of Norway's greatest educators, wrote of Voss: "Here you meet not only ordinary craftsmen and journeymen but also distinguished draftsmen and signet-engravers, clockmakers and even organ builders." Though largely self-taught, this community was also lucid in its usage of language and grammar. Voss has had one poet of unusual talent, Per Sivle (1857-1904). He is not well known in America, but is recognized in Norway as one of its great writers. There's a Sons of Norway lodge at Simco, North Dakota, named after Sivle.

People started leaving Voss by 1750 for northern Norway. It was not until 1836 that organized movements left for America. The most famous Vossing to come to America was Knute Rockne (1888-1931), the great football coach at Notre Dame University. The Rocknes were one of the oldest families in the village and were famed for their skill as blacksmiths and carriage makers. Knute's father, Lars, won second prize at the 1891 Chicago World's Fair with his one-horse carriage. Two years later, when Knute was only five, Lars sent for his family. Knute grew up in the heavily Scandinavian northwest side of Chicago. I had my internship in that community in 1950-1951 and found many people who still remembered Rockne. His pastor said that Knute never forgot him at Christmas, even after he had become famous. A monument honoring Rockne has been erected in Voss, near his birthplace.

Elling Eielsen (1804-1883), who came from Voss as a lay preacher, had a strong impact on the early Norwegian communities in America. His family was influenced by Hans Nielsen Hauge, the farmer who brought a religious revival to Norway that has left a permanent effect on its people. He founded the "Evangelical Lutheran Church in America," known as the "Eielsen Synod." This is the same name chosen for the 1988 merger of the largest denomination of Lutherans in America.

Voss was also noted for politicians in America. The most famous of these was Knute Nelson (1842-1923). After the Civil War, he got a law degree and bought a farm near Alexandria, Minnesota. Elected to Congress in 1883, he became the first Norwegian-born American governor in 1892. In 1895, he was elected the first Scandinavian-born United

States senator and served in that post until his death in 1923. Erling Rolfsrud has written a delightful little book on Nelson named *Scandinavian Moses*.

Ragnvald Nestos (1877-1942) emigrated from Voss with his parents to North Dakota at age 16. After homesteading in Pierce County, he studied law at the University of North Dakota and went into partnership with C. A. Johnson and O. B. Herigstad in Minot. A political conservative, Nestos was elected in 1910 to the state legislature. He was instrumental in obtaining the initial appropriation for the first building at Minot State University and helped secure funding for Minot's first public library. When Lynn Frazier was recalled in 1921, Nestos was elected governor of North Dakota and served until 1924. In 1925, he was a delegate to the League of Nations and was the General Chairman for the visit of Crown Prince Olav and Crown Princess Martha when they visited Minot in 1939. Nestos was inducted into the Scandinavian-American Hall of Fame by the Norsk Høstfest on October 24, 1986. He was also a founder and first president of Minot's Sons of Norway Thor Lodge 67 in 1907.

Though a community of about only 10,000, the people of Voss have been faithful to the best in the Scandinavian heritage and have become a reason for pride among all Americans.

CHAPTER 32

Lars Skrefsrud —
Apostle To The Santals

I FIRST HEARD ABOUT Lars Olsen Skrefsrud (1840-1910) from Rev. Bernhard Helland, a veteran missionary to India, when I attended the Red Willow Bible Camp near Binford, North Dakota, in 1943. I was deeply impressed by his missionary stories.

Skrefsrud was born on a small tenant farm not far from Lillehammer in Gudbrandsdal, Norway. The terrain is rough and his mother feared that he'd stumble on a hillside and fall into the river Laagen below. Lars's father was a skilled carpenter and blacksmith who worked hard and was married to the daughter of a large land owner. Though he made good money, he was a poor provider because of his alcohol addiction. His mother, a devout Christian, was influenced by the farmer-preacher, Hans Nielsen Hauge.

Lars attracted attention at a young age by his excellent answers during the catechizing of children during the Sunday services. By the time he was confirmed at age 14, he had memorized the catechism, Bishop Pontoppidan's Explanation and the Bible History. His mother was his main teacher.

At age 16, Lars left home to work. Then his mother died and his life took some bad turns. He was torn between his mother's teachings and the pressure of his pleasure-loving friends. He had promised her that he'd never touch liquor, but when his friends called him "an old woman," it was too much. Trying to prove himself, he fell in with a drinking group and was involved in a series of burglaries in Lillehammer. The policemen caught him while the others got away. Lars refused to divulge their names and went to prison for 32 months.

This was a time of spiritual despair and lonesomeness. The only person who believed in Lars was a young girl named Anna Onsum, who had been brought up in a Haugean home. Her encouragement restored his hope and he returned to his mother's teaching. He memorized the whole New Testament and taught himself English and German in prison. After his release, he learned Greek, Latin and Hebrew.

In 1862, at age 22, Skrefsrud applied for admission to the mission school in Stavanger. Denied acceptance, he set off for Berlin to enroll in the Goszner Mission School. On the way, he met Hans Borreson, an engineer from Denmark, who became his lifelong friend and colleague. Lars finished the school in one year and had the highest grades in the final examination. He left for India in 1863. Anna Onsum came to India to be his bride in 1865. Mission work among the Santals began in the fall of 1867 at a place named "Ebenezer." Anna died in 1870.

Skrefsrud's missionary methods were based on kindness, not argumentation. He did not ridicule the Santal gods. The Santals were intellectually a bright people, but they had been oppressed by their Hindu landlords.

Skrefsrud was more than a religious teacher. He worked for the economic and social improvement of the Santals. Almost single-handed, he broke the power of the landowners, money-lenders and liquor dealers who had been exploiting the people. Several times they tried to assassinate him. He also pressured the British colonial governor to treat the Santals justly and broke the power of the tribal chiefs who opposed his reforms. To support their work, the mission started a tea farm. (I've tasted the tea from this farm and it is of excellent quality.)

In addition to being an evangelist and social reformer, Skrefsrud was an outstanding educator and was elected to the Asiatic Scientific Society of Bengal. He prepared a grammar of 400 pages and a five-volume dictionary of 700 pages each, the first work of its kind in the Santal language. As a scholar in Sanskrit and Persian, he discovered similarities with Old Norse. He also learned Arabic. The King of Denmark once asked him if it was true that he was fluent in 42 languages. He replied, "Your majesty, it does not depend on how many languages a person knows, but what he says in the languages he knows." The king was satisfied. (While speaking at Luther Seminary in St. Paul, he picked up a Hebrew Bible and read from it as though it were written in his native tongue.)

On trips to Norway, Denmark, England, Scotland and the United States, Skrefsrud was a spell-binding preacher who never used notes.

He could speak for two or three hours with hardly a rustle in the audience. He was ordained in 1881 in the Oslo cathedral. On a trip to Minneapolis in 1891, the Santal Mission Committee in America was organized. The first secretary of the society was Prof. John Blegen of Augsburg College, who organized Bethany Lutheran Church in Minot in 1886. That comes very close to home for me, because I served as Senior Pastor of that church from 1974 to 1989.

Anglican Bishop Stephen Neill, a renowned Christian leader in India, called Skrefsrud "one of the most remarkable pioneer evangelists among simple people that India has ever seen." Kenneth Scott Latourette, the dean of American mission historians, called Skrefsrud "an amazing linguist." His work in India bore rich fruit. There are over 56,000 members in the Northern Evangelical Lutheran Church in India today. That may not seem many in a land of over 700 million in which 83% are Hindu, 12% Muslim and only 2.5% Christian. My friends, however, who have visited the Santals, report that Lars Skrefsrud, the boy from Gudbrandsdal, is still revered among the people to whom he gave his life.

Dr. Olav Hodne has written a brief history of the Santal Church entitled *The Seed Bore Fruit*. It also lists the names of the missionaries from Norway and America who worked in that area of northern India and Bangladesh. It's an exciting story.

CHAPTER 33

Roald Amundsen —
Polar Explorer

W HY WOULD ANYONE TAKE RISKS to accomplish the impossible? Why would anyone be willing to suffer un-told dangers and risk life just to be the first to discover the polar regions? In his book, *My Life as an Explorer*, Roald Amundsen explained what possessed him to make this great effort.

Amundsen was born July 16, 1872, a short distance from Oslo (then called Christiania). His family moved into the capital city while he was only an infant. When Roald was 14, his father died. The older sons in the family went out to work, but Roald remained home with his mother. In accordance with his mother's wishes, young Roald set out to study medicine. One day, however, he read and was impressed by the story of the British explorer, Sir John Franklin, and his search for the "North-west Passage." For almost 400 years, explorers had been looking for a way to the Orient over the top of North America. Amundsen became aflame with the passion to be the one to realize this dream.

To get himself into condition, Amundsen played soccer and skied. He slept with his windows open in the winter to get into condition for the cold Arctic air. He studied hard and graduated from college at age 18.

Despite near-sightedness, he managed to get into the military because of his extraordinary physical condition. The medical doctor "forgot" to check his eyes! As one special test of his endurance, he set out with a friend to cross the mountains west of Oslo on skis in the dead of winter. No one had ever done that before. They nearly froze to death trying and at one time went four days without food before turning back.

Amundsen decided that he needed to become a qualified skipper of an ocean vessel in preparation for his attempt to find the Northwest Passage. In 1897, at age 25, he signed on as First Mate with a Belgian ship heading for the South Pole by way of Cape Horn. For 13 months they were caught in an ice field. Everyone got scurvy and two of the crew went insane. As a result, Amundsen became the ranking officer. Finally, they broke free and sailed into open water for home.

The experience on the Belgian ship proved a valuable preparation for Amundsen's later expedition. He and his party left Norway on June 16, 1903. They sailed by way of Godhavn, Greenland, with 20 dogs on a 72-foot converted herring boat named "Gjoa". They survived many perilous dangers along the way. On Aug. 26, 1905, they sighted a ship from San Francisco named the "Charles Hansson." That was the first anyone knew that they had indeed found the Northwest Passage. It was not until Dec. 5, however, that they reached Ft. Egbert, Alaska, a United States military post. From there they sent telegrams out to the world to announce their triumph. From that day on, Amundsen was a world-renowned hero. On his way back to Norway, he gave lectures across the United States and Europe. Many years later — in 1944 — Sgt. Henry A. Larson of the Royal Canadian Mounted Police became the first person to navigate the Northwest Passage in a single season.

Fame fueled the desire in Amundsen for new conquests. He next turned his attention to trying to become the first person to reach the North Pole. For this expedition he used the "Fram," a polar ship made famous by Fridtjof Nansen. At the last moment he learned that Admiral Robert E. Peary, an American, had already reached the North Pole. (That claim has now been challenged, however). Amundsen changed his plans and left with four companions, 52 dogs, and a four-month food supply to reach the South Pole. An English expedition led by Captain Robert F. Scott was already setting out for the same destination.

Some writers have criticized Amundsen on the grounds that he was not fair to Scott in the race to the South Pole. Amundsen's reply was that he had offered to cooperate with Scott and offered him half of his dogs. Scott, however, preferred to use motorized sledges and Shetland ponies. This was Scott's fatal mistake, according to Amundsen.

Amundsen and his men reached the South Pole on Dec. 15, 1911 (mid-summer in the Antarctic). They planted their country's flag and left letters certifying their discovery. Amundsen's success was made possible because he had planted supplies in advance every three days journey. Scott's group reached the Pole and found Amundsen's claims. On the way back, however, Scott and his crew froze to death. Their motorized units were no match for the Antarctic freeze, whereas Amundsen's dogs endured the cold and provided food for their owners. Amundsen complained that the English were reluctant to admit that the Norwegians had won the race.

In 1925, Amundsen and Lincoln Ellsworth, an American, became the first to fly over the North Pole, using a dirigible purchased from the Italian government. In his writings, Amundsen offered appreciation to Benito Mussolini for his support of these explorations. The Italian leader gave all credit to Amundsen for the success of the venture. Such expressions of appreciation for Mussolini were rare a decade later, but Amundsen did not live to learn the political future of Europe. On June 18, 1928, the famous Norwegian left Tromsø with five companions to search for Umberto Nobile, a famous Italian explorer whose dirigible had gone down. He was never heard from again, though Nobile was rescued.

At the Olav Bjaalands Museum in Morgedal (Telemark), Norway, I learned more about the South Pole expedition. An eyewitness account of Amundsen's discovery has been recorded in *Ski og Sudpol* (*Skis and South Pole*), a book published in Skien, Norway (1970). The book contains, among other things, a number of interesting photographs taken on the expedition.

Al Gimse, a noted Minot skiing enthusiast, shared with me some of his recollections of meeting both Fridtjof Nansen and Roald Amundsen in Minot. His father, Peter, knew both of these famous explorers. He had met them while working in a dry cleaning shop at "Seven Corners" near Augsburg College in Minneapolis. Al related to me that in the early 1920s, both Nansen and Amundsen came to Minot and spoke in the high school auditorium. Al's father was proprietor of the Gimse Cleaners, and Amundsen made the Gimse home his Minot headquarters. Though he had talked with both of these noted men, Al mostly remembers what they said about the importance of skis for their success in polar explorations.

What possesses people to take such risks while others stay comfortably at home? That's a mystery that can only be known by those who take such risks. Most of us are content just to read about the daring exploits of others.

CHAPTER 34

Hans Heg —
Hero Of Chickamauga

HANS WAS ONLY 11 when his family caught "America Fever." His father, Even Heg, and his mother, Siri, were packing their belongings to leave for America. They left their home at Lier, near Drammen, Norway, in 1840 for the New World.

Born Dec. 21, 1829, Hans was soon noticed as an unusually bright boy. He was liked by everyone because of his cheerfulness and patience. In later years, this would make him a leader of men. His father was an inn keeper and knew printing. The Hegs did not go to America because of poverty as so many others did. They had money enough when they left Telemark both to buy land and put up buildings.

Following the usual route from New York, they travelled to Buffalo by river and canal. From there they went to Milwaukee by a Great Lakes steamer. Their destination, Muskego, was only 20 miles to the southwest, a day's journey. There they joined settlers who had come a year earlier.

When Hans was 13, his father built a barn that was to become famous as a shelter for immigrants moving westward. It was also a social center, a church and a hospital. Famous pioneer preachers, such Elling Eielsen, the Haugean evangelist, and Claus Clausen, the Danish schoolteacher, came to the community.

The Norwegians at Muskego held hard views on alcohol. The first Norwegian Temperance Society was organized in the Heg Home in 1848. Hans became secretary and his father the president. Pastor Clausen was often invited to stay at their house. During these years, three dreadful cholera outbreaks occurred. Still the people kept faith with their choice of the New World.

Hans was always on the go. He joined the "forty-niners" in search of California gold. Just when he was doing well, word came that his father died. He returned home to take care of the family farm.

But farming couldn't hold him. Hans had a strong social conscience and became active in the politics of Norway Township and Racine County. He believed strongly in freedom, equality and brotherhood. As a member of the Wisconsin State Prison Board, he did much to improve conditions in the jails and rehabilitation work.

When the Civil War broke out in 1861, Governor Randall appointed Hans a colonel with authority to recruit Scandinavians for the Fifteenth Wisconsin Volunteers. The Irish and the Germans were also doing this. He advertised for recruits, saying: "The government of our adopted country is in danger. It is our duty as brave and intelligent citizens to extend our hands in defense of our country and of our homes." Eight hundred and ninety enrolled, of whom 115 answered roll to the name "Ole." Pastor Clauson became the chaplain and Dr. S. O. Himoe of the community went as the surgeon.

The regiment had only 16 days of training before going to the Southern front. They fought in 25 battles and skirmishes. The battle for which Heg is best known was at Chickamauga, in northeast Georgia, fought Sept. 19-20, 1863. The Union forces were larger but had unwisely divided themselves as they travelled and were ambushed. It turned out to be one of the worst defeats of the Union in the whole war. Heg's men were given difficult ground. They held fast and counterattacked repeatedly. Heg was everywhere. He wouldn't order a soldier to go anywhere that he was unwilling to go.

About sunset on the first day, a Confederate sharpshooter shot Hans in the bowels. He continued on horseback to direct the attack and refused medical aid. Finally, loss of blood forced him to turn over his command to Lt. Col. Ole C. Johnson. He died the next day at noon. When the Union commander, "Rosey" Rosecrans received the news, he wrote: "I am sorry to hear that Heg has fallen. He was a brave officer, and I intended to promote him to be general." Heg was the highest ranking Union officer from Wisconsin to die in the war.

Heg's grave is located close to Norway Lutheran Church on Indian Hill, about 25 miles northwest of Racine. Across the highway is a state park with a museum named for him. There is a statue of Heg with a commanding presence by the park.

Heg had learned English well and I think it quite possible that he might have become the first Scandinavian born governor in the USA, had not war struck him down. Theodore C. Blegen paid Heg this tribute: "The valorous blood of the old Vikings ran in his veins, united with the gentler virtues of a Christian gentleman."

One hundred and twenty years after Chickamauga, I stood in silence before his grave, full of thought. He was only 33. He really loved this land. How often had his wife and children stood there too?

CHAPTER 35

The Korens
Come To America

WHAT WAS A TALENTED and vivacious young girl of 22 doing in a log cabin southeast of Decorah, Iowa, in 1854? Elisabeth Hysing was born May 24, 1832, in Larvik, Norway, to the southwest of Oslo. But in Iowa, among the settlers around Decorah, she was known as "the pastor's wife," and was mistaken to be only 16. One older woman said, "Why, she looks like a mere girl!" A bride of just one year, she was married to Ulrik Vilhelm Koren, the new Lutheran pastor from Norway who would become famous among Norwegians in the New World.

The trip to America began on Sept. 5, 1853. After a brief stop in Hamburg, Germany, they sailed to New York on a three rigged vessel, arriving on Nov. 20. It took another month to reach Decorah. Then they discovered that no parsonage had been built. They had to live with parishioners in one-room log cabins until the following October.

Pastor Koren, born in Bergen, was only 26 when he left Norway. His pioneer work took him to six counties in northeast Iowa plus two in Minnesota. He was one of the first Norwegian pastors west of the Mississippi. Educated at the new university in Oslo, Koren brought highly skilled intellectual gifts plus a zeal for the church to that newly developing wilderness and was a formidable debater. He served Washington Prairie Church until his death, Dec. 19, 1910. It is still a strong congregation.

In addition to his pastoral work, he was a founder of the "Norwegian Synod" in 1855 and its president from 1894 to 1910. He played a major role in the founding of Luther College in Decorah (1861). Today the Koren Library honors his memory on the campus. He was involved in setting up a Norwegian professorship with the Germans at Concordia Seminary in St. Louis (1859). The Norwegian Synod felt a theological kinship with the "Missourians."

NORWEGIAN STORIES: IMMIGRATION PERIOD

The church expected its pastors to visit new settlements of Norwegians and to start congregations. As a result, Koren was frequently away from home. This made life lonesome for Elisabeth. She did not, however, sit around feeling sorry for herself. She was a tireless reader and letter writer. In addition to household duties, diary writing filled many hours. These were later published under the title, *The Diary of Elisabeth Koren: 1853-55*. It was her way of telling Vilhelm what she had done in his absence. I suspect it helped to save her sanity on the frontier too. While her husband was gone, she'd go walking to look for flowers, bushes and seeds to plant, while watching out for snakes. She wrote back to Norway, "You must not be alarmed if you read about Indian troubles." She explained that the "hostiles" lived in western Iowa, while Decorah was in the eastern part.

Elisabeth's diary showed what sort of grit, love and humor was found in those early settlers. The Korens were no ordinary immigrants. They came with a purpose and have left a legacy that is hard to imagine, including their nine children. If you ever visit the Vesterheim Museum in Decorah, you can see some of it it for yourself.

CHAPTER 36

A 'Halling'
Who Showed No Fear

COURAGE AND DETERMINATION have been a way of life for people of the Northlands since the dawn of their history. That spirit of fearlessness followed many of them to the New World. One of these was a "Halling" named Gulbrand Mellem, the first white person to live in Worth County, Iowa. (Hallings are Norwegians from "Hallingdal," to the northwest of Oslo).

Gulbrand built his log cabin on a quarter section of land in 1876 where Northwood, Iowa, now stands. It was a lonesome life. There were no white neighbors for many days journey in any direction. St. Ansgar was their closest town. They waited a whole year to make that trip when they had their new baby, Gustav, baptized.

Those were difficult days for the new settlers in an alien culture. Unfortunately, not all the Europeans in the new land were law abiding and God-fearing people. Some horses were stolen from the Indians by white hunters. The Indians were not about to allow such prairie piracy to go unrequited. A large group of them came to the Mellem farm. They had been told that Gulbrand was hiding the thieves. The Indians dragged him to the barn for punishment along with the culprits. Neither horses or rustlers were found. They put Mellem in the middle of a circle and did a menacing dance about him with knives and tomahawks. The Halling did not flinch. He just stood there with folded arms and looked at them. Realizing that he was innocent, they threw down their weapons and declared him to be a good man. They often stopped in at the Mellem farm for drinks of sour milk and to fill their pipes with tobacco. They remained good friends.

The Norwegians and Indians got along well. It was difficult, however, for these "Native Americans" to distinguish between the "good" whites and the "bad" ones. For the most part, it was the hunters and trappers rather than settlers who got into these troubles. It was not unusual for the Norwegia s settlers to ask the Indians for advice on farming.

NORWEGIAN STORIES: IMMIGRATION PERIOD

Hjalmar Rued Holand (1872-1963) was one of the foremost collectors of stories about early Norwegians in America. His book, *Norwegians In America: The Last Migration*, tells the story of Gulbrand Mellem and many other immigrants. I checked the story out with Mellem's grandson, George (d. 1983), who became one of the best known athletic coaches in North Dakota's history. It was his father that was the first born white child in Worth County. George also told me about his other grandfather, Ole N. Olsgaard, who walked from his farm near Kindred, North Dakota, all the way to Alexandria, Minnesota, to bring grocieries back to his family, over 200 miles round trip.

Few valleys in Norway have sent a higher percent of its people to America than Hallingdal. Courage and the love of having fun were their trademarks. I'm glad they came because my earliest American roots are traced to that valley. So if you have even just a little bit of "Halling" in you, stand tall. It's a great heritage!

CHAPTER 37

Linka Comes
To America

S HE WAS ONLY FIFTEEN WHEN WE MEET HER through the pages of a diary. Being motherless by eight and an orphan at 17 might have crushed many young hearts, but not Linka's. She was a "survivor."

Her diary covered 20 years, from 1844-1864. It was translated and published by a grandson, J. C. K. Preus, in 1952. If I had known what an exciting book this is, I would have purchased a copy before it went out of print. Fortunately, Nora Rogness, a great granddaughter loaned one to me.

Caroline Dorothea Margrethe Keyser was born July 2, 1829, in Kristiansand, on the southern tip of Norway. Her father was a pastor and later a professor of theology. Her grandfather had also been a pastor. "Linka," as she was called, had a good eye for what was beautiful and humorous. She had an excellent education in literature and languages. She loved to read Kierkegaard. More than most Norwegian girls, she travelled extensively and was at home in Christiania (Oslo), Bergen, Kristiansand and Askevold (north of Bergen).

At 21, Linka married Herman Amberg Preus, recently ordained and on his way to become a pastor at Spring Prairie, Wisconsin. The ocean trip took 50 days. Because the parsonage was not ready when they arrived, they had to live in a small and drafty room with a family of the parish. The cultural shock brought many tears.

The diary is a blend of simple faith and profound insight into the mysteries of God. This gave Linka deep humility, endless hope and love for people. As the ship was about to leave Norway, the new bride wrote in her diary: "Hand in hand we go out into the world! Be Thou ever near; we always need Thy help. O Father of all mercies, hear Thou my prayers for the sake of Jesus Christ."

Being the wife of a pioneer pastor required a stout heart and lots of patience. It meant being alone for weeks at a time when her husband

95

travelled to new congregations and to organize the "Norwegian Synod" in 1853. In 1861, he was one of three incorporators of Luther College in Decorah, Iowa. Once in his absence, she had to rescue a calf from the well.

Life on the frontier could be harsh on the women who tended the homes. Only four of her six children survived, two sons and two daughters. From age 27, Linka's health showed the strain of frontier life. When the diary abruptly ended in 1864, she fully expected to die. Yet she lived for another 16 years to age 51.

Linka's life may have been short, but no mother has contributed more children to positions of church leadership among Norwegians in America. Twenty-two sons, grandsons, great-grandsons and great-great-grandsons have entered the ministry, including the Presiding Bishop of the American Lutheran Church, Dr. David Preus. Another great-grandson, Dr.Jacob Preus, was President of the Lutheran Church-Missouri Synod (1969-1981). Besides pastors and bishops, presidents and professors at colleges and seminaries, there has been a governor of Minnesota and a host of daughters who have kept the faith. It was such a mother that the Book of Proverbs (31:28) describes: "Her children rise up and call her blessed." They did and still do.

CHAPTER 38

'Call Her Nettie Olson' — An Immigrant Family's Story

T HE "LITTLE HOUSE ON THE PRAIRIE" was often too small for the immigrant family. This proved to be a challenge to Andrene's family which had emigrated from Hemsedal, a part of Hallingdal in Norway. Like so many others from that valley in the county of Buskerud, they settled first at Blooming Prairie in southeast Minnesota. It is said that all 1400 people living in that city spoke "Halling," besides the many farm families for miles around.

The war between the states was over. Norway, together with other western European lands, had "America Fever." The government was alarmed that so many of its labor force wanted to leave. The State Church issued warnings to the people about the dangers which they faced if they went to that uncivilized and heathen land. If they escaped being mugged in New York, they would surely be met by "Savages" waiting for their scalps on the prairies and in the woodlands. They were forcefully advised that they would be leaving behind both family and God, if they went to America.

Threats did not keep people from seeking passage to the New World. They bought the cheapest fares. For about $50 or $60, a person could travel from Norway to Iowa and Minnesota. There were tears as the last glimpse of the "old country" faded from their eyes. Later they would sing, "Kan du glemme gamle Norge?" ("Can you forget old Norway?") After a brief stop at Newcastle and Liverpool, England, they saw no land until they docked in New York City's harbor.

There were no fond memories of their quarters in the steerage section of the boats. The food was equally bad and it did no good to complain. To the shipowners, immigrants were simply "cargo," not much different than if they had been cattle. Nor were they safe from attacks by the ship's crew. Women stayed in the protection of their men. The smell and disease were sickening, not to mention rats. It was not uncommon to die at sea in such conditions.

NORWEGIAN STORIES: IMMIGRATION PERIOD

Ole and Kari Bakken were among those who came to Blooming Prairie in 1867. Their name had been "Hølle" in Norway. They settled on a farm near the Red Oak Grove Lutheran Church. Andrene was the youngest of their six children. One Sunday, they were visiting the nearby farm of Uncle Knute and Aunt Guri. When it was time to go home, Andrene, just six years old, was nowhere to be found. After an anxious search, she was discovered asleep in the tall grass by the railroad tracks.

Now Knute and Guri had no children. Their only child had died. This was not an unusual thing in those days. Guri was the one who found the missing Andrene. When she returned with her to the farm, she announced: "Because I found her, she is going to be my little girl. Besides, you already have enough children!" Nothing would change her mind, Andrene would replace the child that had died. Finally, Ole and Kari yielded. They thought it might be good for Guri to have a little girl in her home. Besides, the Bakken house was getting crowded. Andrene, however, wasn't happy with the arrangement. It didn't take her long to decide that what Aunt Guri really wanted was someone to do the chores. She'd run home to her parents so she could play with her sisters. Then Guri would come with a stick and order her to return.

The Bakkens had three sons and needed more land. This was not easy to find in the Blooming Prairie community. In 1879, they moved to a site west of Walcott in southeastern North Dakota where many other Hallings were settling. Their oldest daughter, Anna, remained behind to be married. Andrene chose to stay with her. This was a happy period in her life. When it came time to enroll in school, a neighbor girl took her along. She was asked by the teacher, "What is your friend's name?" After a pause, she answered, "Call her Nettie Olson." And Nettie Olson it was for many years. She was a good listener and had a deep love for learning. She had a special ability for memory work and qualified herself to be a teacher.

There wasn't much "romance" to life on the prairie in those days. It was mostly harsh survival. Houses were built without insulation and stood as stark silhouettes against the horizons. It took years before the groves of trees grew up to give protection against the elements. Conditions were far different from Norway. The summer heat was intense. Bugs, flies and other insects were everywhere. Milk soured quickly and it was impossible to make cheese or butter when gnats filled the air. Lightning storms were particularly loud and frightening. Rattlesnakes were often found in the fields. The greatest terror came from prairie fires. In the dry weather and with a hard wind, it took no time for a field to become a sea of flames. The fires moved so quickly that the fastest horse could not outrun their fury. Travelers carried matches to light backfires as a way of protecting themselves. The winter blizzards also tested the endurance of the strongest settlers and there was very little money.

The Red Oak Church became a source of inspiration for Andrene. She memorized long sections of the Bible and loved to sing hymns, ballads and folk songs which she had learned by heart. One of the famous pioneer pastors was in the Blooming Prairie community from 1875-83. He was Rev. Claus Clausen. A native of Denmark, he ministered among Norwegians. Earlier he had been at Muskego, near Milwaukee, one of the earliest Norwegian settlements in the New World.

Andrene married Hellik Thoreson (renamed Thompson) from Lyngdal in Numedal, west of Oslo. After living a few years by Doran, Minnesota, they moved near her family by Walcott, North Dakota where they reared seven children. When she was married, she reclaimed her name, "Andrene," but I will always affectionately remember her as "Grandma."

CHAPTER 39

Knute Nelson —
Champion Of Children's Rights

KNUTE NELSON (1843-1923) WAS THE first Norwegian immigrant to become a state senator, congressman, governor and U.S. Senator in the New World. In Washington, Nelson used his influence to enact some of the most significant legislation ever to become law in our land.

Who was Knute Nelson and what kind of a beginning did he have? Born in the district of Voss at Evanger, Norway, his mother brought him to America in 1849 when he was only six years old. For a short time they lived in the new city of Chicago, but times were tough and they moved to La Grange, Wisconsin. There his mother married Nels Nelson, also an immigrant, and Knute was given his new father's name. In 1853 they moved to Deerfield, about 20 miles east of Madison.

When Knute was 15, he entered nearby Albion Academy where he worked for his tuition and room. He brought food and fuel from home. Then he taught school. When the war between the states came, he enlisted in the Union Army and fought at Vicksburg and New Orleans. Later wounded, he was a prisoner for a month.

After the war, Knute studied law with a lawyer in Madison and was admitted to the bar in 1867, the same year he was married. Politics drew him into public life, beginning with the state legislature in Wisconsin. In 1871, he moved to Alexandria, Minnesota, frontier country in those days. Combining homesteading and law, he was soon back in politics, becoming county attorney and a state senator. Washington beckoned Nelson to Congress in 1882 for three terms. Then he quit. But in 1892, the Republicans elected him governor to try to keep the Scandinavians from joining the Populist Party. Elected twice, he resigned when named by the legislature to be a United States Senator. He was re-elected until he died.

When Theodore Roosevelt was president, the Nelson amendment to a bill establishing the Department of Commerce and Labor began

100

sweeping reforms in child labor laws. Roosevelt wanted authority to publicize information about the wrongdoings of large corporations. John D. Rockefeller sent telegrams to six key Senators opposing the bill. The bill passed the House by 252 to 10 on Feb. 10, 1903.

More than 1,500,000 children worked for as little as 25 cents a day in 1900. In one case, a mother reported: "The boss was good; he let me off early the night baby was born." In three days she was back at work with the baby in a little box on a pillow beside the loom. Children of six became wage earners and snuff sniffers. There is evidence to claim that much of America's wealth in the 19th century was bought at the price of children's toil. When confronted, the owners threatened to close the mines and mills.

Nelson, a short man of broad stature and whose chin whiskers turned gray early, became known as the "grand old man of Minnesota." He lived a simple lifestyle. Not only Minnesota, but the nation is in debt to this immigrant boy. In his lifetime, he was the best known Norwegian in America. Today his statue stands in front of the State Capitol in St. Paul.

Norwegian Immigrant Children.

CHAPTER 40

T. G. Mandt — 'Wagonmaker'

MANY PEOPLE KNOW THAT Stoughton, Wisconsin, has been called "The most Norwegian city in America," but few may be aware of the man who brought it so much fame. His name was T. (Targe) G. Mandt. Born in 1845 in Telemarken County, Norway, he came to Dane County, Wisconsin, when just two years old.

During the Civil War, Mandt wanted to join the army, but was too young. So he went to St. Joseph, Missouri, and got a job making wagons for the Union forces. He became so good at it that after the war he moved to Stoughton and began making wagons to sell. Only 19 and with just $40 in his pocket, he was convinced that he could build a better wagon than anyone else. According to thousands of farmers in Wisconsin, Minnesota, Iowa and the Dakotas, he did.

During the years 1873-75, hard times came to the farmers. Grasshoppers descended like a biblical plague. It looked like the end for Mandt as the creditors came to collect. He didn't have bankruptcy laws to protect him, but Mandt wouldn't have used them anyway. Because of his good reputation, the creditors agreed to take 35 cents on a dollar. Even though he had his receipts marked "paid in full," Mandt paid his creditors every cent he had owed when the business bounced back. It was that kind of honesty that went into making his wagon a quality product.

It wasn't long before the wagon works became Stoughton's busiest business. This is also the reason why so many Norwegians flocked to this city which still has one of the best "Syttende Mai" (17th of May) celebrations in the nation. By 1883, 225 men worked for Mandt. Then tragedy struck. On Saturday, January 13, 1883, fire destroyed almost the whole plant. It looked bad for everyone in the city.

But Mandt was not a quitter. He had been travelling when the plant burned. Upon his return, he gave orders to rebuild immediately. Within a week, orders were being filled again. His massive frame and seemingly endless human energy set a good example to all his workers. He was also generous and gave frequent gifts to charity. On Christmas Day 1901, he collected $500 for the orphan's home in just a few hours.

As a manufacturer of wagons, sleighs and carriages, Mandt's motto was "The Best is the Cheapest." People used to say they could tell a Mandt wagon when they met it because it didn't rattle. In the last year of his life, he built 15,000 wagons and sleighs. He died Feb. 28, 1902. The people of Stoughton remember their famous citizen with pride. If you drive past there sometime while travelling between Madison and Chicago, take an hour or so to visit this fine community.

I remember the wagons. In the fall, we'd put our Model T up on blocks. Wagons and the sleighs were our transportation to town as well as what got me to school on many cold mornings. I thought those were fun times. Sometimes I feel we lost something pretty good when we put away that equipment which was built with such honesty and charm. They were a little slow moving, but we had a ringside seat to prairie life as we rolled along those trails.

CHAPTER 41

'Snowshoe' Thompson
Carries The Mail

BEFORE THE "PONY EXPRESS" carried mail over the Sierra Nevadas, a young Norwegian from Telemark sailed on skis across 90 miles of stormy heights from Placerville, California, to Carson Valley, Nevada. For twenty years, John A. Thompson, known as "Snowshoe" Thompson, carried the mail over the mountains to isolated camps, rescued lost people and helped those in need. He was a legend in his own time.

Born April 30, 1827, he emigrated to America with his mother when he was ten. After living in Illinois, Missouri and Iowa, he joined the gold-seekers in California when he was 21. He was lonesome for the mountains. Anyone who has been in Telemark knows how much mountains are a part of the people's lives.

Having moved to California, Thompson bought a ranch in the Sacramento Valley. He didn't care for a miner's life. His is believed to be the first farm owned by a Norwegian in California.

He read about the difficulty of getting mail across the Sierras and volunteered for the job. Made from oak trees on his farm, his skis were over ten feet long and weighed 25 pounds. People laughed at them and said they wouldn't work. Today they are in a Sacramento museum.

Thompson skied up to 45 miles a day over snowdrifts 50 feet deep with a load of 60 to 100 pounds on his back. Travelling light, he carried only some crackers and dried meats to eat. He did not use liquor, but scooped up snow to drink if no mountain stream was nearby. Wearing just a mackinaw, he had no blanket to keep warm. More than once Thompson jigged until morning to stay alive. Nor did he carry a weapon for protection against wolves or grizzlies. Once eight wolves blocked his path. When he didn't flinch, they let him pass. The stars and his wits were his compass.

Snow in the Sierras was deep, sometimes higher than the trees. Many mornings Snowshoe had to dig himself out of a snow bank to continue his journey. When travelling to Washington, D.C., in 1874, the train became stuck in snow so that four locomotives could not pull it through. He took to his skis and in two days had travelled the 56 miles to Cheyenne, Wyoming, beating the train.

What was his pay for 20 years of work? Many promises, but the government's response was, "We're sorry, but . . ." Later investigation into the Postmaster General's records indicated that they had not even noted his name, only his route and the dates.

For all his fame, he was a modest man, never boasting or sitting on his haunches. He is regarded today as the the most remarkable man to have ever buckled ski straps in America. One postmaster claimed he saw Thompson jump 180 feet without a break. When just 49, he died of a liver ailment on his California ranch. He is buried in Diamond Valley, 30 miles south of Carson City, beside his only son who died at age 11.

Thompson is still remembered by family in America. Janet Erdman of Willow City, North Dakota, wrote me that her grandfather, John Sanderson, was Showshoe's nephew. Like so many children of immigrants, they're proud of their Scandinavian heritage and glad to be Americans.

CHAPTER 42

Rasmus B. Anderson
And King Frederick's Pipe

R ASMUS B. ANDERSON (1846-1936) was proud of his pipe. It had once belonged to Denmark's King Frederick VII. But Anderson's story is a proud chapter in Scandinavian American heritage, even without the pipe.

He was born in Koshkonong, one of the two earliest Norwegian settlements in Wisconsin. His father had owned a small trading vessel in southwest Norway. He was a born rebel. Besides being a "Quaker," he helped promote "America Fever" in Norway. Rasmus' mother was from a prominent military family, as her name "Von Krogh" might indicate. Her grand-uncle was the commander of the Norwegian armies. When she married a peasant, there was nothing to do but go to America.

Jens was only four years old when his father died of cholera, which descended upon communities like a plague in those days. His mother was a cousin of Mrs. A. C. Preus, the wife of a pioneer Koshkonong pastor. Through her influence, young Rasmus entered the first class of Luther College (1861) when it was called "Half Way Creek Academy" in Wisconsin. The school had a Spartan beginning. The parsonage served as the campus. A boy's school, the students all slept, dressed, wrote, recited and visited in one upstairs room.

Humble beginnings need not be a limiting factor for a person's growth and development. There are many of us who got our early education in one-room country schools. It was there that Rasmus began the study of languages, math, history, literature and other courses that were to prepare him to become the first Scandinavian in America to be appointed to a diplomatic office. He became the U.S. ambassador to Denmark in 1885. He was also a distinguished professor at the University of Wisconsin.

While in Copenhagen, Anderson became friends with a Jewish writer named Adler, who had bought a pipe at an auction that once belonged to King Frederick VII. When he was about to return to America, Adler gave it to him as a present.

106

How did the pipe come to be sold? Usually these things are kept as mementos and put in museums. King Frederick VII had expected to be Norway's first king after the constitution was signed May 17, 1814. But the British had forced the Danish king to sign Norway over to Sweden after the Napoleonic wars. So Christian Frederick, as he was called, had to return to Denmark and wait his turn to become king there. He did one remarkable thing. He gave Denmark a constitution in 1848, like the one he helped Norway to obtain. It surprised people because the Danish kings were "absolutists," rulers without a constitution.

The royal family wasn't a bit pleased when he married a dressmaker. She had all the natural qualifications to be queen, except blood line. It was a happy marriage. When they died, their possessions, soiled by the hands of a commoner, were sold at a public auction.

Anderson understood the royal snub, since his mother had also fallen from favor by marrying below her class. So when a good friend came to visit him, he'd hand him the royal pipe and say, "Take a puff and be a king."

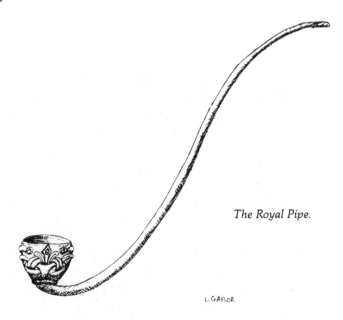

The Royal Pipe.

L. GAYLOR

CHAPTER 43

Jens Hanson And
The Vatican Library

JENS HANSON WAS ONLY NINE in the summer of 1873, when a relative from America was visiting in Valders. The visitor, Rev. Ove Hjort of Paint Creek, Iowa, asked Jens' father, a government official, to send one of his seven children back with him to America. Jens was selected to make the trip and was promised that he would be able to attend Luther College in Decorah. Thirty-four years were to pass before he would return to Norway. He never saw his parents again.

Travelling through Chicago, Jens kept a wary eye for bandits, for even at that time they had an international reputation. Arriving in Decorah, he was given private instruction. The following year, he was admitted to Luther College at age ten. That may be a record for the school. Though young, Hanson remembered college with a great deal of fondness, especially sports.

In 1882, Jens went to study at Concordia Seminary in St. Louis. It was common in those days for the Norwegian Synod students to study at the Missouri Synod school. But after two years, he realized that he ought not be a pastor. So he took a job teaching in a Norwegian parochial school on Chicago's northwest side. One time, he arranged a wrestling match between a Chicago champion and a member of the church's Young People's Society. Being the only one present who knew the rules of modern wrestling, he was also the referee. For this he was severely criticized in a Norwegian language newspaper.

Hanson's education continued at Cornell University. There he studied history under some of the best professors of the time. He was also Cornell's star baseball pitcher. These studies led to his joining the staff of the University of Wisconsin in 1893. From there he became chief cataloger at the Library of Congress in 1897. In 1910, Jens joined the University of Chicago Library staff where he rounded out his career.

One of his most interesting assignments was four months in 1928, when he was loaned to the Vatican Library in Rome to introduce the Library of Congress cataloging system. Upon arrival in Rome, the Americans were given a private reception by Pope Pius XI, who himself had once been a librarian. When the Pope learned that his guests spoke German, he talked very openly and cordially to them. The Vatican Library is the world's richest treasure house and is said to occupy more than 11,000 rooms!

Hanson enjoyed Rome. Since the International Bibliographic Congress was to meet the following year in the Eternal City, he was asked to serve as one of 11 delegates on the planning committee. Imagine his surprise when he found out that two of the others were not only from Norway but from Valders!

One of the strange things about Hanson's story is that when Jens first arrived in America, he wrote letters to his family pleading that he be sent home to Norway "by mail." Who can guess what is in store for a child? Hanson reorganized five major libraries and is the chief author of the cataloging rules used today throughout the world. What a loss to the world would have occurred if his parents had sent him a return ticket.

CHAPTER 44

Knute Reindahl —
Violin Maker

SCANDINAVIANS HAVE BEEN VERY fond of wood carving and music. These talents met in Knute Reindahl. Born in Telemark in 1858, his father died when he was just three years old. He had come from a family of silversmiths who were always carving wood as well. On his mother's side, an uncle was considered the best rosemaler (ornamental painting) in Norway. Her name, Gulbek, was also found on the finest violins in the land. His great-grandfather was the king's bodyguard in war and was thought to be the strongest man in Norway. He used to break up feuds at wedding parties. That's how he met his death by an iron bar over his head.

When Knute was nine, his mother emigrated to Madison, Wisconsin. A boat accident in the Skien harbor made her wish she had never left. Times were tough for immigrants in America. She worked in the harvest fields and his sisters worked as hired girls. Yet he remembered these as the happiest days of his life. Knute got little schooling. He never passed beyond the fifth grade, even though he was a year older than his teacher. He'd rather carve salad bowls and picture frames than study in books. Selling his hand-made trinkets, he visited the Indian camps on Lake Monona by the city. They taught him how to make bows and arrows.

Realizing that wood carving was his chief interest, Knute returned to Norway in 1887 to study ornamental carving. He had learned that the best violin makers had originally been woodcarvers. He also tried his skiing skills in the mountains of Telemark. Trying to outjump his brother, both skis fell off and he landed like an arrow into the soft snow.

Success in America did not come quickly, but hard work and determination had its rewards. When the Chicago Symphony moved into the newly built Orchestra Hall on Michigan Avenue, the old violins built by masters were too weak to be heard. The Director bought five of Reindahl's violins in their place. In 1900, the Reindahl Violin won the

110

Diploma of Merit for woodcarving and had a special medal struck for it at the World's Fair in Paris. He was the only violin maker mentioned in the "Who's Who" of the World's Columbia Exposition in Chicago.

One of the dreams of a violin maker is to discover the "lost art of the masters." One of the great swindles in musical instruments is people who claim to have made this discovery. Knute contended that the only magic was good workmanship. His wood was spruce from the ruins of a 14th century stave church near Oslo. How good were his instruments? In 1922, when the city of Madison wanted to honor Fritz Kreisler, they presented him with a Reindahl Violin. Nothing less would do for the "master."

A Danish violin teacher by the name of Adamsen, who had studied in Italy, said of the Reindahl Violin: "I am surprised that anybody can make that good a violin here in America." One writer has described Reindahl as "the outstanding artist in wood among Norwegian Americans." The artist's comment about his life was: "I was always whittling." And through his hands, personality passed into his works of art.

CHAPTER 45

The Saga Of
Torger Skaaden

MOST OF THE RECORDS about immigrants to America have been lost forever. I know very little about the inner feelings and exact thoughts of my ancestors from Norway. They've not left so much as one written word for their families.

That makes the journalling of Torger Johannesen Skaaden significant. I was fortunate to examine a copy of his chronicle called *My Life's Adventure* or *Experiences in the School of Life*. It was translated by Carl C. Damkaer of Upham, North Dakota, in 1920.

Skaaden was born November 28, 1836, in Norway, the son of Johan Skjonsberg and Ingeborg Skaal. He was the oldest of nine children. He wrote that his father was "not very religious," but his mother "more religious." She "taught us prayers and hymns which I will never forget."

His earliest memories were of a brother, Amund (who died at age five), a pair of sealskin pants and his first day at school. He remembered being told at bedtime to say prayers, cross himself three times and then "safely lie down and go to sleep."

Skaaden's early education consisted of lessons taught by an itinerant teacher who went from farm to farm, staying a week at each place. Among the documents which attracted him was the Norwegian constitution of 1814 from which he came to believe that the king in Stockholm was "holy."

He remembered his confirmation instruction from Pastor Nissen whom he called "an exceptionally good minister." He did not, however, get the religious "high" that he had expected from confirmation.

Today we plan our lives almost as if we were going to live forever. It was different in Torger Skaaden's world. Epidemics ravaged communities. There were many large families, but few who did not bury several children. It was common for a man to be married at least two or more times. Childbirth, hard work, unfriendly weather, lack of medical care and economic hardship separated many mothers from their families.

This also happened to Torger Skaaden. His first wife, Karen, journeyed with him to America and died within a year of arrival. Ingeborg, a ten-year-old daughter, became mother and housekeeper for the family which included a six-month-old child. Their first home in America, a 12 by 12 cabin with a dirt floor, did not offer many luxuries. Then Torger married Lisbet. Sixteen years later (1903), she also died. By this time they had homesteaded in McHenry County of North Dakota, having first settled in the Goose River Valley in eastern part of the state.

In 1906, at age 68, Torger returned to Norway to visit his family and friends. To his regret, most of them were no longer alive or still in the old home community. He had returned too late.

His journals told of crop failure which drove him to consult a Swedish pastor named Frantsen who advised him to tithe from his income. One night by candlelight, he read of a family in Minnesota whose house had burned down. They had lost everything. He was so moved that the next morning he got on his pony and collected 85 dollars for the unfortunate people. He observed that "the one who has the hardest time is the most willing to give."

World War I weighed heavily on the minds of the immigrant families. Like so many people, he was fascinated by the Book of Revelation, finding parallels in its descriptions to the early 20th century.

Death was an ever present shadow on the immigrant communities. He wrote: "I have seen death come in many different ways - at times quietly and peacefully, at other times with great struggle as when it came to our Master on the cross and he called out, 'My God, my God, why hast thou forsaken me?' " His early childhood training in the Bible comes through over and over again in these writings.

The story of Skaaden's struggles were not only concerned with economics, diseases and death. It was also the inner struggle of faith against the fatalism that comes from contemplating the sovereignty of God. Torger could resign himself to God's ultimate authority, but yet he struggled with the issues of life.

Like so many immigrants from Norway, his political convictions were to the "left." "Populism" was popular among these folks whose sense of nationalism in their homelands was strong. Constitutionally guaranteed freedoms and the right of self-determination burned in the hearts of these newcomers to America.

Skaaden's journal is no literary masterpiece, even though it shows a sensitive appreciation for good literature and poetry. There is much left out that the reader would like to have known about dates and places. The significant thing is that he wrote these journals at all. One wonders what he might have done with a college education. I think he might have gone far. He had a sense of vision to life and reflected meaningfully on his experiences. His family is richer for these memoirs. These writings are not the rambling thoughts of a barbarian, but of a man with a highly cultured soul. I wonder how many more of these prairie prophets have passed our way unnoticed.

CHAPTER 46

'Apaurak'
In Alaska

I READ HER OBITUARY with special interest: "Alaska missionary dies at age 90." It referred to Dagny Brevig Nimmo who died Jan. 19, 1987, in Maine. My mind flashed back to my freshman year at Concordia College in Moorhead, Minnesota, 43 years earlier.

Concordia's Professor J. Walter Johnshoy had just written a book entitled *Apaurak In Alaska: Social Pioneering Among the Eskimos*. It describes the work of Rev. Tollef Brevig (1857-1935) among the Eskimos above the Arctic Circle in the areas of Teller, Igloo and Shishmareff from 1894 to 1917. I bought the book because of my high regard for the author who was my academic advisor in a philosophy major as well as my Hebrew instructor. I've had many outstanding teachers, but few have inspired me to study as much as Johnshoy. I felt a deep loss when he died suddenly at the beginning of my senior year in 1947.

Who or what was "Apaurak?" It's an Eskimo name for "Father of All" and was given to Brevig by the Eskimos in a special ceremony. He was the only pioneer white missionary and social worker in Alaska who was adopted into an Eskimo tribe. Born in Sigdal, Norway, Brevig emigrated to America at age 10 with his parents. After graduating from Luther College in Decorah, Iowa, he taught school for 11 years in Minnesota. Then he enrolled at Luther Theological Seminary in St. Paul, graduating in 1891. During March, 1894, while serving as a pastor in Crookston, Minnesota, Brevig received a letter from Rev. Herman A. Preus, president of the Norwegian Lutheran Synod, asking him to consider going to Alaska.

The United States government wanted to help the Eskimos get started in raising reindeer. Siberians had been employed for two years but they were cruel to both Eskimos and reindeer. The government wanted to import Lapps (Sami) from Norway, known to be the finest reindeer herdsmen in the world, to come to Alaska. The Lapps, however, agreed to come only if a Norwegian Lutheran pastor lived among them to minister the Gospel. Brevig arrived in Alaska, Aug. 1, 1894, accompanied by his wife, Julia. He didn't know that he'd also be the manager of the reindeer herds and Teller's first postmaster.

Brevig was the first schoolteacher in the area. He found that the Eskimo children were quick to grasp concrete concepts but they had difficulty with abstract reasoning. Because they counted on their toes and fingers, numbers over 20 gave them trouble. Brevig quickly learned the Eskimo ways and the people felt a strong sense of trust towards him because his word was always good.

The fur traders and whalers tried to keep missionaries away. Knowing that the missionaries would protect the Eskimos from exploitation, they said, "Next spring men will come with a book which they say cannot lie and which is given by God. These men who bring the book are liars and the book itself is full of lies." It didn't take the Eskimos long to figure out who the real liars were.

Some of the early encounters of the Eskimos with foreigners had been a disaster. Many of the Russian government officials were extremely cruel. The U.S. purchase of Alaska in 1867 eventually brought better times. The Eskimos were, for the most part, a trusting people with a strong sense of justice. Their religion, however, was centered in spirit worship, controlled by the "shamans" (witch doctors). Their living conditions were anything but sanitary, with poorly ventilated homes and lice everywhere. Bathing was not one of their virtues. They thought water was only for boats and had no appreciation for soap.

Christmas became a high point among Eskimos in Teller after Brevig's arrival. They journeyed 70 miles into the interior to fetch the first Christmas trees. The annual Reindeer Fair brought people together for competition. The U.S. Commissioners and Marshalls were busy protecting the herds from poachers. In the early days, ships with supplies and mail were scarce. Sometimes it took a whole year to get news from home.

Professor Johnshoy, as a little boy in his father's parsonage, had known Brevig. When Brevig died, his journals were given to Johnshoy for editing and publishing. A highly qualified linguist and a master of style, he put together an exciting story. It tells of Brevig's experiences during the "Gold Rush" days (described in Rex Beach's books), of intense cold, treacherous travel across the snow and ice, disease and death, struggles with those who wanted the missionaries out, competition from some later missionaries and the satisfaction of seeing the Christian faith as well as better living conditions take root in an aboriginal people.

Brevig's wife and two children died in Alaska. He returned to mainland USA several times to promote the mission's work. At age 56, he returned again to take over the work when no one else would go. Later missionaries included Bertha Stedje of Hettinger, North Dakota, who went out in 1945, and Pastor Albert Tastad of Rolette, North Dakota, from 1953 to 1956. Dagny "Alaska" Brevig, to whom the book is dedicated, worked with her father as a schoolteacher and helped with the mission orphanage until 1917. With her recent death, the last of the original missionaries to that far corner of America has come to an end.

Great work is usually done by a few dedicated people, not the masses. Brevig and his family dared to be those kind of people. He well earned their title, "Apaurak, Father of All."

"Apaurak" — Missionary Brevik.

CHAPTER 47

Some Early Norse
Settlers In Montana

WHO IS THE GREATEST Norwegian to have lived in America? Writing at the turn of the last century, Martin Ulvestad pointed to Knute Nelson, the famous senator from Alexandria, Minnesota, as the best known, but he claimed that Anton M. Holter, pioneer of the lumber industry in Montana was the greatest business entrepreneur among Norwegian-Americans. Holter came to Helena, Montana, in 1863 at age 32 and was the first of his countrymen to settle in the state. He urged other Norwegians to follow. At that time, most of the settlers in Montana lived in the mountain areas, on both sides of the Great Divide.

Montana wasn't an easy place to live back in those days. Fierce snowstorms took a terrible toll on the cattle and sheep. As late as 1884, bandits were still robbing the mails and rustling horses. (I remember visiting in 1945 with an early Bozeman pioneer who told me about the Gallatin Valley vigilantes.) There was no effective law enforcement, so it was done by the citizens. T. S. Norgaard moved from Minot, North Dakota, to Helena, a city of 25,000, to edit *Montana Folkebladet* (a Norwegian newspaper). Gold mining, real estate, banking, lumber, retail and contracting attracted 1,400 Scandinavians to share in the new wealth. Danish-Americans published the *Montana Statstidende*.

Martin T. Grande came to America from the Trondheim area, in 1866 at age 22. Arriving first in Minnesota, he travelled by stagecoach through Salt Lake City to the Helena area in 1877 to pioneer the Montana sheep industry. That was the year of the Nez Perces Indian uprising. When the wool dealers in Helena refused to pay the prevailing six cents per pound, Grande shipped his wool by riverboat to Boston and got 30 cents a pound. In just a few years he owned 12,000 sheep, many horses and cattle, and 17,000 acres of land. Not afraid of hard work, he also labored in mines and hunted wild game, while keeping a sharp eye out for Indians. Grande became so famous back in Norway, some Norwegians thought he must be President of the United States. One of his descendants, Ray Grande, attended Concordia College at Moorhead, Minnesota, in the early 1940s where he became a football star.

The first Norwegian congregation in Montana was Melville Lutheran Church in the Big Timber area, established in 1885. Another early one was Our Savior's Congregation in Helena organized by the Norwegian Lutheran Synod in 1890.

Helena was full of Texas steers and cowboys in those early days. Gun fighting took place on a regular basis. The last Indian uprising occurred in 1890. The immigrants fortified themselves when a message came from Camp Crook in South Dakota that Sitting Bull was about to attack. It was only a rumor, however, Sitting Bull was killed the night after the message arrived.

The story of Endre Bergsagel, born near Stavanger in 1890, is quite another tale. He came to the Larb Hills southwest of Malta, Montana, in 1913. The Bergsagels were highly respected people in their homeland. His father, Daniel, served on the school board and was a county commissioner. The oldest of seven children, in 1910 he sold some land and, together with his brother Knut, bought a ticket to America.

Bergsagel described the journey in his memoirs published by the Norwegian-American Historical Association. Many immigrants from Norway took a steamer to England and entered the New World through Canadian ports. Bergsagel went on to San Francisco where an aunt helped him get his start in America.

After working in various odd jobs for three years in western United States and Canada, Endre went to the land office in Malta to claim a homestead. Luckily, the first winter was mild and open. He had to travel 35 miles to Malta for lumber to build his first shack (8 x 10 with tarpaper sides fastened with lathes). The furnishings were simple: a cast iron stove, a table, a chair and a folding bed. In the summer of 1914 his fiancee, Gurina, arrived from Norway. She was in for a surprise. It was not just the wide open spaces of prairie land, but mosquitoes! They were married by Pastor Alfred Hendrickson in the Malta parsonage, with a lunch served by the pastor's wife following the ceremony.

It was not an easy life. The war in Europe caused them deep concern. Rationing and other regulations were in effect. Then the flu epidemic of 1918-1919 took many lives. Gurina became ill, but fortunately recovered. In 1919, the Bersagels rented out their farm and returned to Norway for five years.

They returned to the farm, and things looked great for a few years. They were active in building both a church and the local schools. Then came the Great Depression. 1932 saw drought, grasshoppers, cutworms and webworms. By 1933, they moved west to Poulsbo, Washington. They returned for a last look at the farm in 1941, but were not tempted to stay. They became part of that great throng of midwesterners who crossed the mountains to live nearer the ocean, the natural habitat for Norsemen.

Many more stayed behind. During the summers of 1946-1949, I worked among Scandinavians from Culbertson, Bainville, Fairview, Sidney, Richey, Lambert and down to Glendive. They're good people. I'm glad they stayed in Montana.

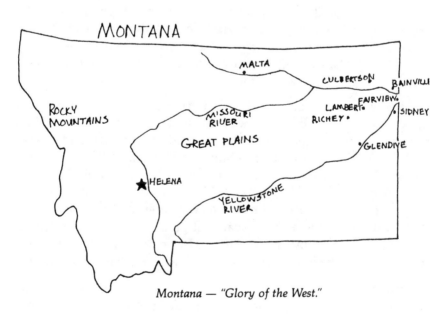

Montana — "Glory of the West."

CHAPTER 48

Poulsbo, Washington —
Norse Home In The West

I SHOULD HAVE REALIZED when I bought a loaf of "Poulsbo Bread" that it came straight from the heartland of a Norwegian settlement. Not only did it have a Viking ship design on it, but it reflected the tastes of those hardy Northmen.

Poulsbo, Washington, a city of about 4,000, is located north of Bremerton on Puget Sound. The very name "Poulsbo" means "the place where Paul lives." There are a couple of theories about how the city got that name. Some say it was named after Iver Moe who had come from Norway. He was one of the town's first settlers. It has been suggested that the postal authorities misspelled the name on the application for a post office, the intended name being "Paul's Bo." Another theory is that it was named after a Paul Wahl. Whatever it was, the city has retained its strong Norwegian character since its founding in 1886.

If you've ever travelled in the Seattle and the Puget Sound area, you can understand why this place attracted Scandinavians. Poulsbo appeared as a Norseman's paradise with the forests and lumber industry, the water and fishing, but without the harsh winters of their homelands. Many of the early settlers wrote back both to Norway and to Minnesota urging their friends and relatives to become a part of this new community.

The idea to write this story was given a boost when I went to give farewell greetings to Betty Rogstad as she retired from the *Minot Daily News* and prepared to move back to Poulsbo. Betty had grown up in that community and was now returning home. She tried to convince me that Poulsbo is even more Norwegian than Minot and sent me a packet of information to prove it. I am also indebted to a good friend from college and seminary days, Peter Tengesdal, formerly from Maxbass, North Dakota. Peter was pastor of First Lutheran Church in Poulsbo from 1967 to 1987.

The church was one of the first institutions to be planted in Poulsbo. The Norsemen organized "Førdefjord Menighed" in 1886, now known as "First Lutheran." Lutherans in America are fond of calling their congregations "First," something unknown in their homelands. They learned it from their American Protestant neighbors. In 1897, when the "Friends of Augsburg" broke away from the United Norwegian Lutheran Church in America to form the "Lutheran Free Church," emissaries were sent from Minneapolis to Norwegian communities to organize new congregations. Thus a second Norwegian congregation called "Grace Lutheran" was organized. That's also how Zion Lutheran Church in Minot, North Dakota, was started.

Another interesting connection for me to Poulsbo is that Rev. A. M. Lunde, who was pastor of Our Savior's Lutheran Church in Colfax, North Dakota, during my childhood, later located in Poulsbo. My father's confirmation certificate carries his signature. He died in 1946.

The roster of names in the early days of Poulsbo would make you think you were right back in Norway or North Dakota. Names like Borgen, Eliason, Fatland, Hagen, Iverson, Langeland, Moe, Myrvang, Nilsen, Tallagson, and Vik, not to mention the Andersons, Johnsons and Olsons, reveal the ethnic heritage of the community. The list of men inducted into the military during World War I sounds like the roster of a Norwegian regiment. Several of these men served in France.

During World War II, when Norway suffered under the Nazi occupation, the people of Poulsbo supported the Norwegian relief efforts. They continued doing so after the end of the occupation as Norway began to emerge from the ravages of war. They publicly saluted the courageous people of Finland who sent over $500,000 in cash and supplies within a one-month period to Norway, despite their own hardships resulting from the Soviet invasion. The Finns also sent more than $200,000 worth of medical supplies to Norway which were needed in Helsinki.

In 1905, the people of Poulsbo received with enthusiasm the exciting news that Roald Amundsen and his crew had discovered the "Northwest Passage." They eagerly awaited the arrival of his ship to Seattle the following summer and gave him a tumultous welcome upon his arrival.

The Sons of Norway organization has a strong chapter in Poulsbo. In 1973 they built "Grieg Hall" to preserve their heritage and to serve as a home for their many activities. One of the interests of the townsmen is to have a model Norwegian city built using architecture like that found in the Old Country at the turn of the past century. Poulsboites also celebrate a "Viking Fest" for three days around "Syttende Mai" (17th of May), when Norway remembers its constitution of 1814.

Just to illustrate how "Norwegian" the Poulsbo folks feel themselves to be, a poll was taken in 1969 asking for suggestions for a community theme. Seven hundred fifty-seven residents responded "Little Norway" and 382 said "Scandinavian." So "Little Norway" it has been.

The city is growing too. At the beginning of World War II, Poulsbo had 639 residents. By 1960 it reached 1,505, by 1970 it had 1,856, and by 1980 it had grown to 3,453. And it's still growing.

In 1975, Poulsbo was honored by the visit of His Majesty King Olav V from Norway. The King was in nearby Seattle, the home of a large and active Norwegian-American settlement. People of that area also attend the Norsk Høstfest in Minot. The Viking Fest and the "Little Norway" theme have rallied the people of Poulsbo to take pride in heritage.

Poulsbo, of course, is not exclusively Scandinavian, even though their Chamber of Commerce brochure has the words "Velkommen til Poulsbo" on the front cover and "Welcome to Little Norway" on the inside. In addition to the Viking Fest, annual events include the "Midsommar Fest" (Midsummer Festival), a lutefisk dinner in October and a "Yule Log Lighting Ceremony" in early December. They've also erected a Viking statue on the waterfront. The map of the North Kitsap Peninsula area contains many names that show that this is a Norse home in the West. "Velkommen til Poulsbo" is this town's invitation to the world.

CHAPTER 49

The Spring Grove
Norwegians

"VELKOMMEN TIL SPRING GROVE" (Welcome to Spring Grove) is the headline on the brochure describing a famous Norwegian-American community in southeast Minnesota. Spring Grove claims to be the first Norwegian settlement in Minnesota. They hold a three-day celebration in May to coincide with the "Syttende Mai" (17th of May) festival, which commemorates the Norwegian constitution of 1814. They've been celebrating this event annually since 1971.

Norwegians began moving into Fillmore and Houston counties in 1852. Lars Tollefsen of Hallingdal, Norway, brought his family to Riceford, just inside the Houston County line, that year. When the railroad by-passed Riceford in October 1879, Lars moved some of the buildings into Fillmore County to the railroad where the town of Mabel was established just seven miles from Spring Grove. Riceford then became a ghost town. The Tollefsens had previously lived a short time in Wisconsin.

The following year, Norse settlers started coming in caravans. A few years later, many of them moved to the Dakotas and Montana. There were quite a few Fillmore county people in the Wolford, North Dakota, community. One of the churches of those early settlements was named "Bloomfield." (There's also a Bloomfield Church at Upham, North Dakota, and one north of Glendive, Montana, near Lindsey. My earliest roots in America come from near Blooming Prairie, a short distance to the west of Spring Grove. After a dozen years, my great-grandparents moved to Walcott, North Dakota. It was the typical pattern of early immigrants.)

The Spring Grove folks plan an interesting weekend for visitors in their Syttende Mai festival. They have a quilt show, a parade, some "Big Stakes Bingo," arts and crafts, a Fiddler's Bee, some historic bus tours, evening entertainment, and a Norwegian church service on Sunday with a dinner served by the local Sons of Norway. Hikers may like to go on the "Folkemarsj," a 10 or 20 kilometer walking trail through some of their most scenic countryside.

A local genealogist, Georgia Rosendahl, is on hand to help people discover their Scandinavian origins. She has traced the roots of the earliest settlers to the present descendants. Georgia's father-in-law, Peter Julius Rosendahl (1878-1942), who farmed near Spring Grove, produced the "Ola og (and) Per" cartoons from 1918-1935. They were printed in the *Decorah-Posten*. I'm indebted to Georgia for some of the information in this story.

Since Decorah, Iowa, is only 22 miles away, they offer a trip to Vesterheim, the most prestigious Norwegian-American museum in North America. Just another 50 miles away is Norskedalen, near Coon Valley and Westby in Wisconsin. Norskedalen is a 350-acre site nestled in the palisades of the Mississippi River which looks a lot like parts of Norway. Tours were arranged to visit the Steam Engine Museum in Mabel. The steam engines draw about 35,000 people on Labor Day weekend for an old time thresher's show. It began in 1953 on the Gerhard Clauson farm near Hesper, Iowa.

The Spring Grove folks also offer a tour of the Amish community near Harmony. Over 100 Amish families live there. Besides farming with horses, they make quilts, baskets, furniture and other crafts to sell. One of the host farms has a barn built by Mr. Allis of the Allis-Chalmers company. The famous racing horses, Dan Patch and Tommy Briton, were raised here. Nearby is the largest limestone quarry in southern Minnesota.

Syttende Mai isn't the only celebration these Scandinavian enthusiasts of southeast Minnesota hold. In July they put on Rodgers and Hammerstein's "South Pacific." The production takes place in Ye Olde Opera House, a community theatre. In addition to reserved seating, people bring blankets and sat under the stars while listening to "Some Enchanted Evening." A "Fall Foliage Festival" is held in October. Anyone who has taken a drive along the Mississippi in early October knows what a feast of color it is to the eyes. They call this the "Bluff Country." But by whatever name it's called, this is a delightful place of American beauty.

NORWEGIAN STORIES: IMMIGRATION PERIOD

Spring Grove is near Burr Oak, Iowa, the home for the "Little House on the Prairie." Laura Ingalls Wilder's books have their setting in this area. There's a historic site named after the famed author in Spring Grove.

There are caves to visit in the area. Mystery Cave is near Spring Valley and Niagara Cave is near Harmony. For people who want to know more about the early settlers to the area, the Fillmore County Historical Centre in Fountain is open Monday through Friday.

Trinity Lutheran Church in Spring Grove was organized in 1855 by the Norwegian Synod with 700 souls. That was a pretty big membership for a beginning congregation. They had grown to 1,200 by 1914. Among those 1,200 were four Swedes, a German and an American. Trinity is a congregation with vision. Not only did they have a ten-acre cemetery, but they had an additional 60 acres of farm land. In 1893, they built a brick church that cost $20,000. Their first parsonage cost $5,000 in 1858. The Spring Grove Norwegians took a lot of pride in their church. Today they have over 1,600 members in a town of less than 1,300. Besides Trinity, there are many more congregations of Norwegian origin in the Spring Grove area which are active to this day.

How did it happen that so many Norwegians found their way to southeast Minnesota? After Cleng Peerson's famed voyage in his sloop named the "Restauration" in 1825, whose passengers settled in upstate New York, later Norwegian immigrants went to the Fox River Valley west of Chicago. They kept on moving, however, and soon were in Racine County, Wisconsin, and in the Madison and LaCrosse areas. They came in such large numbers that there wasn't land enough for them in the earlier settlements. They'd stay with other Norwegians, often people from their home communities in Norway. A barn was not considered a bad place to sleep as they moved on to their eventual destinations. Always they heard the stories of more land for less money out west.

They were fortunate for the most part. The land purchased near Indian Hill, southeast of Milwaukee, was no paradise. But if you drive through that area today you will find beautiful farmland with well kept buildings. They did better in their land purchases in western Wisconsin and in Minnesota. My father told me that some were too eager for land as they came to the Dakotas. Many came in the winter when snow covered the ground and were victims of sharp land agents. The sales pitch often turned out to be much better than the soil. Once purchased, it was too late. They were deep in debt. Still, many of them stuck it out and did well, despite drought, rocks, grasshoppers, hailstorms and disappointing grain prices.

So if your Norse roots should have a Spring Grove connection, you'd enjoy visiting with these good friends at one of their festival times. For more information, write Karen B. Gray, 222 Highway 44E, Spring Grove, MN 55974. The people of Spring Grove have not forgotten their heritage. May their kind continue.

Norwegian flag.

CHAPTER 50

Ole Evinrude And
The Outboard Motor

NORSEMEN HAVE ALWAYS LOVED the sea. So it isn't surprising that they turned their inventive abilities to design the longship — and, many years later, the first commercially successful outboard motor. Water recreation was revolutionized by the work of Ole Evinrude.

Evinrude, whose name has become well known to everyone in the recreation business, was born on April 19, 1877, 60 miles north of Oslo, the oldest of 11 boys. When Ole was five, the family went to America and obtained a homestead near Cambridge, Wisconsin. But farm life was not for this adventurous young Norseman. As a teenager, Ole built a sailboat which was the talk of the community. At age 16, he walked the 20 miles to Madison, where he became an apprentice machinist in a farm machinery factory. From there he went to Pittsburgh and then Chicago, learning everything he could about steel and motors.

In 1900, still only 23 years old, he opened a shop in Milwaukee while serving as the master pattern-maker and consulting engineer for the E. P. Allis Company. He studied internal combustion engines and manufactured portable motors.

On a hot Sunday afternoon in August, 1906, while on a picnic near Milwaukee, Ole's girlfriend, Bess Cary, said she wanted a dish of ice cream. Dutifully attentive to her wishes, Ole rowed five miles round trip to get the ice cream. Even for a big, strong man like Ole, this was a test of emotions. While pulling the oars, he began to think about mounting motors on boats, and thus began a revolution in recreation.

In 1909 he and Bess, now married with a son, started the Evinrude Company. Ole was the inventor and engineer, Bess took care of the office and wrote letters to promote the business. "Throw away the oars," was the slogan she used. Business, however, was tough. People weren't convinced about the new "putt-putts." The letters and circulars finally paid off. A Danish employee of a company with a Scandinavian department

128

saw the Evinrude circular in the general manager's wastebasket. Starting with two motors, the firm increased its orders to thousands as Scandinavian fishermen clamored for the new invention. After three years, Evinrude was employing 300 people and building a new factory.

Both Ole and Bess worked hard and put in long hours. Because of Bess's failing health, Ole sold his share in the Evinrude Company in 1914 to his business partner with the agreement that he was not to start up a new company for five years. The family went off on a trip to the west in a large Packard that Ole had customized. They also cruised on a 42-foot boat over the Great Lakes.

Ole, however, kept on tinkering and designed a two-cylinder motor. Bess's health improved and they started the Elto Outboard Motor Company in 1921, named from "Evinrude Light Twin Outboard." In 1929, a merger of the Evinrude Company with the Elto Company and the Lockwood Motors of Jackson, Michigan, resulted in the Outboard Motors Corporation with Evinrude as president and the largest stockholder. Competition was tough. Evinrude's company and the Johnson Company competed for the market. Evinrude stressed lightness and was the first to use aluminum in the motors. The Johnson Company stressed speed, up to 16 miles an hour! Then came the Great Depression. Ole offered the best buy. He sold a motor for only $34.50, F.O.B. Milwaukee, and managed to stay in business through the worst of those times.

Again Bess's health weakened and she died in 1933. Ole's spirit failed without her and he died just 14 months later on July 12, 1934, at age 57. His only son, Ralph, gained control of the Johnson Motor Company after it became bankrupt in 1932. It was merged with the Outboard Motors Company in 1936 to become the Outboard, Marine and Manufacturing Company. By the early 1940s they were making 60% of the outboard motors sold. Today the company is known as the Outboard Marine Corporation with headquarters in Milwaukee.

What kind of a person was Ole Evinrude, the boy who emigrated with his parents from Norway? He was remembered as a shy person whose formal education ended with third grade. He didn't care for farming, but was a mechanical genius in everything that required the use of hands. His favorite subject was arithmetic. While in Madison, he went to night school to learn algebra, calculus, trigonometry and engineering.

He even made his own automobile and built a gasoline engine. Hard work and long hours brought on severe rheumatism. It got so bad in the winter that he had to go to bed, but he'd take his drawing board with him to keep on designing.

Two other outboard motors had been built before Evinrude's, but Ole was the first to produce one that was commercially and mechanically successful. The Evinrude product is now used around the world. The James Bond movie, "Live and Let Die," used an Evinrude on the 110-foot boat making its escape in the final scene. They've come a long way since the original single cylinder built in 1909!

Ole's son, Ralph, lives in Jensen Beach, Florida, where he is married to Frances Langford, the former actress. He has been associated with the company since 1927, after attending the University of Wisconsin. The next time you go for a ride on a motorized boat, remember the shy Norwegian boy who changed the world of water sports.

The outboard motor.

CHAPTER 51

The 'Friends
Of Augsburg'

MANY PEOPLE ASSUME that the warring spirit of the Norsemen became peaceful when they accepted the Christian gospel. This has been true in military matters of modern times. It is significant that Norway furnished the first Secretary General for the United Nations in the person of Trygve Lie. The Nobel Peace Prize is also awarded in Oslo.

The warrior spirit of the Vikings, however, is not dead. It has taken new directions. Norwegian immigrants always seemed ready for a good fight in politics and religion.

In the late 19th century when the Scandinavians were winning a high percentage of county and state offices in the New World, an intense church struggle occupied the immigrants. As a result, competing Norwegian Lutheran congregations were established in many communities which challenged each other's ministries.

The historic doctrines of the faith were not at stake. It was rather the role of laymen, freedom of congregations, liturgical practices and the emphasis on Christian experience rather than doctrine. The pietistic movement led by Hans Nielsen Hauge was a powerful influence on these people.

The struggle went back to the Old World. The farmers in Norway were rising to assert their rights. The constitution of 1814 encouraged self determination in all areas of life, including the church. What right or competence, for example, did secular authorities have to appoint bishops and pastors?

It was a time of church merger among the immigrants. In 1890, the "United Norwegian Lutheran Church in America" was formed by three groups: The "Conference," the Norwegian Augustana Synod and the "Anti-Missouri Brotherhood." The Hauge Synod was not included in the merger, neither was the Norwegian Synod, which was closely related to the Missouri Synod.

131

The agreements for merger went well. However, at the last moment it was discovered that St. Olaf, rather than Augsburg, would be the official college of the church. Augsburg was to continue as the official seminary. This posed a threat to Augsburg's integrated educational program to prepare men for the ministry as the seminary included both a college and a high school.

Augsburg's faculty, known as the "New School," was progressive in its educational views. They opposed transplanting a European system for training pastors among the immigrants. Little love was lost between St. Olaf and Augsburg during those days. St. Olaf charged Augsburg with having an inadeqate educational program and Augsburg claimed that St. Olaf was tainted with humanism. Besides, could the church afford two colleges?

As a result, the Augsburg administration, led by Georg Sverdrup and Sven Oftedal, refused to turn Augsburg's property over to the new church. As the situation grew more tense, a group of people calling themselves "Friends of Augsburg" met in June, 1893 to plan their defense. The United Church, led by President Gjermund Hoyme, wanted to force the issue and started Luther Seminary that fall. Twelve congregations were expelled from the United Church, including Trinity, located near the Augsburg campus.

At their annual conference at Pontoppidan Church in Fargo in June, 1896, the Friends of Augsburg gathered for their last ditch stand. In the meantime, the United Church had started court proceedings to gain control of the Augsburg property. At their annual meeting in June, 1897, the "Friends" met at Trinity Church in Minneapolis to organize the "Lutheran Free Church" (LFC). About 125 congregations with 6,250 members made up the dissenting group. (My mother was confirmed in one of these congregations near Doran, Minnesota, called "Sticklestad" named after the battlefield where St. Olaf was killed). The Minnesota Supreme Court ruled on June 21, 1898, that the United Church had no legal claim to the Augsburg property. Augsburg Publishing House, however, did revert to the United Church. The "Friends" had done their job well.

Bethany Lutheran Church in Minot had been organized by the Augsburg faculty in 1886. When the split took place, Bethany remained in the United Church but its pastor went with the LFC. Shortly afterwards, Zion Lutheran Church was organized in Minot as a new LFC congregation.

It wasn't until 1963 that the schism was repaired when all but 51 congregations and 6,000 members joined the then American Lutheran Church and today are mainly found in the newly formed "Evangelical Lutheran Church in America" (1988)! The modern day dissenters formed the "Association of Free Lutheran Congregations."

I had frequent contact with the LFC since my high school days. The first Bible camp I attended in 1943 at Red Willow Lake was under LFC auspices. As a result, I attended Oak Grove High School in Fargo for my senior year. Oak Grove had been organized in 1906 as the "Oak Grove Ladies Seminary." My wife, Gerda, attended Augsburg College in 1950-1951 while she was Assistant Health Nurse at the college.

The LFC members later referred to the Norwegian Lutheran Church in America (NLCA) as the "big church." It was organized in 1917 by another merger which included both the Hauge and Norwegian Synods. The LFC and the NLCA drew closer together as a new a generation of leaders led both groups. They cooperated closely in world missions and relief work, evangelism, youth work and in many other areas. In the light of past events, it was significant that the final LFC Annual Conference was held on the St. Olaf College campus in 1962.

A great deal of credit for this reconciliation has to be given to the LFC leadership: Dr. Bernhard Christensen, president of Augsburg from 1938 to 1963; Dr. T. O. Burntvedt, president of the LFC from 1930 to 1958; and Dr. John Stensvaag, president of the LFC from 1958 to 1963. (One of the friends of our family, Dr. Olai Sletten, pastor of St. Olaf Lutheran Church in Minneapolis, was president of the LFC from 1920 to 1923.)

It was Shakespeare who said, "All's well that ends well." We can say that now, but the rift among Norwegian Lutherans was a bitter time for the immigrants. I'm told that my grandfather, Ole Fiske, who immigrated in 1892, strongly opposed the LFC.

In his book, *The Lutheran Free Church*, Prof. Eugene Fevold lists among the reasons for the split "Norwegian stubborness." Dr. Edmund Smits, a Latvian professor who came to teach at Luther Seminary after

World War II, told me that this "stubborness" can be a valuable asset when rightly directed.

Like America itself, it has taken the Norwegians in our land a long time to understand their life in the New World. "Freedom" is a priceless possession and should never be surrendered lightly. "Trust," however, is even more priceless and should be cultivated with great patience and even pain. The "Friends of Augsburg" were true to their convictions and were an honorable and gifted people. Their legacy lives on in the Scandinavian heritage today.

Augsburg Seminary — Minneapolis.

CHAPTER 52

Norwegian Deaconesses
Build Hospital In Chicago

MUCH HAS BEEN WRITTEN about the strong character of Norwegian women in the Viking period and during the Middle Ages. This strength continued on in the Norwegian deaconesses who came to Chicago at the turn of the century.

Chicago was a popular stopping off place for immigrants from Scandinavia. The area around Humboldt Park and Logan Square, northwest of the Loop, is dotted with churches started by these newcomers to America.

This metropolis of the Midwest had some rough and tumble sections. It was into those places with poverty, hardship and crime that a group of young women set out to build a hospital, start a school of nursing and reach out to families in need. They had a special concern for orphans, unwed mothers, the aged and drunks on skid row.

The deaconess movement began in Kaisersworth, Germany, in 1836, under Theodore Fliedner who established its famous motherhouse. Florence Nightingale learned nursing there. It became the model for the deaconess programs throughout Europe and America. Several of the leaders in Chicago came from the motherhouse in Oslo. The head of the local order was called both "Mother Superior" and "Sister Superior." The members were called "Sisters." The name "deaconess" means "one who serves." It's a work that goes back to biblical times. Many sisters became nurses, others became social workers, parish workers and some missionaries.

Having been turned out of the first Norwegian hospital built in Chicago, the sisters did not give up. They organized a society in 1896 which became a part of the United Norwegian Lutheran Church of America. Beginning in rented quarters, they opened the Norwegian Lutheran Deaconess Home and Hospital in 1902 on Leavitt Street. H. B. Kildahl was the first rector (chaplain). The hospital continued until

1969. But this was not the end. A new medical center named Lutheran General in suburban Park Ridge, one of the finest in Chicagoland, is the successor to the deaconess' work. I was a teacher at the new hospital from 1967 to 1972 and we have a daughter-in-law who graduated from the School of Nursing.

My first contact with the Chicago Deaconess Hospital was as a seminary intern at Bethel Lutheran Church near Humboldt Park in 1950-1951. I was with a group of students invited to a Halloween party. One Deaconess in particular, Sister Magdalene Klippen, was the life of the party. It was only later that I learned of her fearless courage and her compassion for the poor of the city. A *Chicago Sun Times* newspaper reporter wanted a story on Sister Magdalene's skid row work, but insisted on having police protection as he followed her around. The skid row residents, however, had great affection for her. She was their "angel."

Sister Ingeborg Sponland (1860-1951), born in Norway, was Superintendent of the hospital for 20 years. She spent 66 years in deaconess work and is remembered for saying, "As a deaconess, speak with your hands. Good honest work is the best sermon." Well said. These great women represented the best of the Scandinavian heritage.

Norwegian Deaconesses in Chicago.

CHAPTER 53

Ole Rølvaag —
A 'Giant In The Earth'

H E WAS ONLY 55 WHEN HE DIED IN 1931. But the boy from the island of Donna near the Arctic Circle had become world famous. Ole Edvart Rolvaag was born April 22, 1876. Six generations of the family had lived on this rocky, wind-swept and treeless cove.

Fishing was the main business of the community, but Ole's father was also a good carpenter and did some small farming. They grew barley, rye, potatoes and raised a few cattle and sheep. The chief interest of the Rølvaag family, however, was literary. By age six, everyone was expected to start reading. This did not come easy for Ole. Formal education began at age seven. There were three terms of three weeks each during the year. The only road to the schoolhouse seven miles away was a rough path. School ended with Confirmation at age 14. Then he was off to apprentice with a fishing captain.

Fortunately, Ole did learn how to read well, but it was the storytelling during the long winter nights that stirred his imagination. When he read *The Last of the Mohicans*, a story about life in the New World, a new idea began to take root in his mind. After a terrible sea storm off the Lofoten Islands, where many sailors were drowned, Ole resolved to go to America. An uncle at Elk Point, South Dakota, sent him a ticket. His employer offered to buy him a sleek new fishing boat if he would forget about America. Ole stuck to his plans.

After working on his uncle's farm in South Dakota, Ole decided that milking cows and cleaning barns was not the job for him. Afterall, that was women's work in Norway. A pastor encouraged him to get an education. At age 23, Ole entered Augustana Academy at Canton, South Dakota. He graduated in two years with honors. There he met Jennie Marie Berdahl, the daughter of a pioneer family, who later became his wife. It was from her relatives that he received much of the information about pioneer life. In the fall of 1901, Ole began his studies at St. Olaf College. He did so well that Pres. Kildahl wanted him to become a pastor. But Ole decided he would be a teacher and a position was offered him at St. Olaf where he remained for the rest of his life. During the summer of 1904, he taught parochial school at Bisbee and Churches Ferry, North Dakota.

At St. Olaf, Rølvaag had a double career as a professor and a writer. He was always a close friend of students in need. It was during these years that he wrote his most famous book, *Giants In The Earth*. His tragic hero, Per Hansa, is immortal to all who have read this novel. It was a Book of the Month Club selection in 1927. *Peder Victorious* and *Their Father's God* completed the trilogy.

Though he was of only modest stature and suffering from heart problems in later life, it was pride and will power that propelled the boy from the windswept island of the North to become a "giant." On the St. Olaf campus, the library memorializes this professor who has given us the most vivid description of immigrant life among the Norwegians on the Dakota prairies.

Many people called "giants" are misfits in society. Rølvaag, however, was known by his friends as one who loved life. He has added much to our appreciation for living.

CHAPTER 54

General L. J. Sverdrup —
'Engineer Soldier At His Best'

"**E**NGINEER SOLDIER AT HIS BEST," this is how General Douglas MacArthur described the son of a Lutheran parsonage who immigrated to America from Norway at age 16. Leif Johan Sverdrup is possibly the most honored Norwegian to have lived in the New World.

How did this immigrant boy from the west coast of Norway attain to such fame? He arrived in America on Dec. 7, 1914, sponsored by a relative, Jorgen Heiberg, of Twin Valley, Minnesota. To begin with, he worked on farms in the area and even taught "parochial" (religious) school. At age 18, he entered Augsburg College in Minneapolis and earned a bachelor of arts degree in two years. After serving in the U.S. Army in World War I, he earned another degree, this time in engineering at the University of Minnesota. His first job was with the Missouri State Highway Department where he proved his ability that was later to become so famous. It was not long before his engineering professor, John Ira Parcel, joined him in forming Sverdrup & Parcel and Associates, Inc. which became one of the world's largest and most respected engineering and architectural firms. The headquarters are in St. Louis.

By the time of World War II, Sverdrup had become world famous. In August 1941, the State Department asked him to build a chain of airstrips in the Philippines which could land B-17s. MacArthur expected a Japanese attack by April 1942, when the monsoon season was over. When Sverdrup delayed his answer, he was told, "You gotta do it." He went and did a job which still defies belief.

Sverdrup never did get to the Philippines on that trip. The Japanese arrived first. But he did build a chain of airfields that moved the U.S. planes to victory up through the South Sea islands. One of the most interesting stories told of his many exploits and how he got the runways packed hard enough to land the big planes. According to the *St. Louis Post-Dispatch*, "He would send his native interpreter ahead to a new village to announce that a supernatural man was coming. Then Sver-drup would march in carrying his wind-up phonograph. The awed natives built his airfields by day and were rewarded with dances at night. Shortly after the last pair of dancing feet had padded down the new airfield and had gone home to rest, the airplanes would come roaring in."

Sverdrup built more than 200 airfields and related military projects. It is no wonder that General MacArthur stated on Jan. 12, 1945, on a heavy cruiser in Lingayen Gulf: "This is the engineer soldier at his best."

After the war, Sverdrup continued his energies for peace as a devoted family man and to rebuild downtown St. Louis. He had a great deal to do with developing the city's famous riverfront which includes the Arch and the Busch Memorial Stadium. The Boy Scouts of America awarded him their highest honor, the Silver Buffalo. By this time, he had become a personal friend of presidents and kings.

On a trip to the nation's capital, he noted that there was no statue of St. Olaf in the Washington Cathedral. The Sverdrups commissioned a sculptor and presented a memorial to Norway's patron saint.

I had not lived long in St. Louis, having arrived in late 1961, when people began to tell me about the famous Norwegian who had become a legend in their city. The Sverdrups, of course, had already distinguished themselves as one of Norway's best known families. They were leaders in government, church, Arctic exploration and scientific research. They had come to America too. Both an uncle and a cousin of Leif had been presidents of Augsburg College and Seminary. He never lost his love for Norway, serving as the Norwegian Vice Counsul in St. Louis. He was known to say that the "shortest distance between two points was through Norway." He returned often.

My first appointment with this famous Norseman was on Oct. 1, 1962. I asked his support to promote a concert by the St. Olaf Choir the following February. I was not disappointed. He made me feel at ease with his natural friendliness. He offered his help and with one phone call to his friend, Richard Amberg, Editor of the *St. Louis Globe-Democrat*, I had a story in the newspaper.

We met several more times, once in our home. At his funeral on Jan. 5, 1976, messages were read from President Ford and King Olav V. It was fitting that at such a service the congregation should sing, "A Mighty Fortress is our God!" MacArthur was right! And his legend lives on.

CHAPTER 55

Knute Rockne — An Untold Story

OR THE SCHOOL YEAR 1950-51, the faculty of Luther Theological Seminary assigned me for an internship to the Logan Square and Humboldt Park areas of Chicago's northwest side. It was a pretty big change for a North Dakota farm boy who had never planned to live in a city larger than Minneapolis, and then only for going to school.

It turned out to be an exciting year and I'm still glad for the experience. It was an unexpected education. This area had a heavy concentration of Scandinavians at the beginning of the century. There were still quite a few left when I was there 50 years later, but many had moved out to the suburbs. Today, Spanish is the most common language in this community, now populated primarily by Puerto Ricans.

This was the community where Knute Rockne (1888-1931) had grown up, and there were still people living at the time of my internship who remembered him. This immigrant lad from Norway, who made Notre Dame's "Fighting Irish" famous for football, became better known than any president or graduate of the school. When I lived in Glenview, a northern suburb of Chicago from 1967 to 1973, I had a friend who was a Holy Cross priest from Notre Dame. He loved to talk about the famous exploits of Rockne on the gridiron.

Later, as a pastor in New Rockford, North Dakota (1957-61), I ministered to the wife of Theodore J. Lund, who had confirmed Rockne. Lund was pastor at the Hauge Lutheran Church near Logan Square. The Rocknes were members of another "Haugean" church named Immanuel. Immanuel Church had a pastoral vacancy when Knute was in confirmation so Lund helped out. Mrs. Lund shared with me some things which are not well known and which I have not found in any of the written biographical material about him. Lund was in Chicago from 1900-1904. He became pastor of the former Hauge Lutheran Church in northeast Minot in 1912. (The white frame church still stands but is an

142

apartment building today.) Huldas Peterson of Minot remembers Lund well. She went to Sunday school at the Hauge Church when he was the pastor.

The Rockne story goes far back into Norwegian history. When Queen Margaret I forged the Union of Kalmar in 1397, uniting Norway, Denmark and Sweden into one great North Sea power, an ancestor of Knute Rockne named Enidride Erlandson opposed the treaty and moved to Voss in the western mountains of Norway. That's how the Rockne family got identified with Voss. It's an unusually beautiful place, and if you go there today you'll find a monument in Knute's honor.

The Rocknes were an inventive family. Knute's great-grandfather was the first farmer in that part of the country to build and use a farm wagon (with wheels) instead of using a sledge. Knute's grandfather was a blacksmith and hardware merchant and was said to be handy with machines. His father, Lars Knutson Rockne, became a popular builder of two-wheeled vehicles. Germany's Kaiser Wilhelm, who vacationed at nearby Balestrand every year, bought one of them. The English also liked to vacation in Norway's western mountains, and one of them, a nobleman, talked the elder Rockne into going to Chicago to exhibit his buggy at the 1893 World's Fair. He won a prize at the fair — but, more importantly, he liked Chicago so well that 18 months later he and his family decided to make their home in the Windy City.

Knute wasn't cut out to be an artisan. He grew up as a tough street kid who learned how to use his fists, even though he was small. The ethnic rivalry between the Scandinavians and Irish often was resolved on a vacant lot, with an Irish policeman named O'Toole standing watch. If the Norskies got the upper hand, he'd stop the fights. Knute's friends petitioned the city to send them a Swedish cop. At full growth, he stood just 5'8" and weighed only 145 pounds. He grew up in a pious family whose life was centered in the church. The entire family was musical. Knute's instrument was the flute, which he later played in the Notre Dame band.

Rockne did well in all sports but was expelled from high school for cutting too many classes. He went to work at odd jobs about the city, went harvesting in Wisconsin, and spent four years working for the Chicago Post Office. By then he'd saved a thousand dollars to go to

143

college. He picked Notre Dame over the University of Illinois because some friends persuaded him that it would be a good school. He also figured it would be cheaper for him. So on Nov. 28, 1910, at the age of 22, Knute resigned his postal job and enrolled at Notre Dame.

Until that time, the "Irish" hadn't done much in football. It had been Notre Dame's practice to take boys off the farm and boys from poverty areas and help them to get an education. The school for boys began in 1844 in such a state of poverty that it got its Indiana charter only with the help of a Methodist friend. The big day came at the Army-Notre Dame game in 1913, when Knute was a senior. Army was rated as the team to beat that year, and the game was expected to be lopsided. Rockne, as team captain, changed football forever in that game by introducing the forward pass. Later he was to introduce the platoon system. These tactics totally confused the game plan of their opponents and the Irish went on to defeat the Cadets and shock the sports writers.

Knute planned to become a physician, so he took a heavy load of math and sciences. His transcript is impressive and he graduated magna cum laude — not bad for a high school dropout from an immigrant family. Upon graduation he became a chemistry teacher who laid the groundwork for the invention of synthetic rubber. How then did he become a football coach? According to his grandson — Knute Rockne III, who coaches a sophomore team at Bright High School in Midvale, Utah — Notre Dame offered him $5 more and he needed the money. His record as head coach (1918-1930) is well known: 105 wins, 12 losses and 5 ties. His teams had five undefeated seasons. He is still the winningest coach the Irish have ever had.

He guided some great players. George Gipp was immortalized by the phrase, "Win one for the Gipper." Jimmy Crowley, Elmer Layden, Don Miller and Harry Stuhldreher became known as the "Four Horsemen." (The other players on the team were called the "Seven Mules.")

For many years Rockne was known as the "lone Norse Protestant" on the Notre Dame Campus. On Nov. 20, 1925, he joined the Roman Catholic Church, perhaps out of deference to his wife and children, according to Mrs. Lund. She told me that he continued to remember her husband, who had confirmed him, with a Christmas present each year until Rockne's death in a tragic air crash in 1931.

Those who knew Rockne well had high respect for him. He had a great sense of humor and frequently told jokes about himself, but in such a way as to cause others to think about themselves. If you ever visit Voss in the beautiful mountains of western Norway, be sure to visit his memorial near the railway station. It will warm your heart.

The 1988 Norsk Høstfest honored Rockne by posthumously inducting him into the Scandinavian-American Hall of Fame. He was represented at the award ceremony by his daughter, Mary Jean Kokendorfer of Tulsa, Oklahoma.

Knute Rockne.

145

CHAPTER 56

The 'Ola And Per' Comics

FROM 1918 TO 1935, PETER JULIUS ROSENDAHL (1878-1942), a farmer from Spring Grove, Minnesota, produced the comic series "Olga og Per" ("Ole and Peter"). It had a large readership, even though often produced only in the off-seasons.

The first paper to carry the series was the *Decorah-Posten*, well known among Norwegian-American immigrant families. The cartoons were used to increase their subscription list. The paper reached a circulation of 45,000 during the 1920s, but dropped to 35,000 by 1950. In 1972, the subscription list was sold to the *Western Viking* in Seattle which continues to reprint them. When I asked my mother if she had read "Ola og Per," she gave an immediate recollection.

Born of Norwegian immigrant parents, Rosendahl also wrote poetry and song texts. Besides drawing cartoons, he painted portraits. He travelled very little and his only formal training was a correspondence course in cartooning from a school in Minneapolis. His father was from Hadeland, near Oslo, and his wife was a Halling. These places were also the backgrounds for the two main characters. Ola, the Halling, wore overalls and carried a pitchfork over his shoulder. Per, the Hadeling, appeared in a long-tailed suit and carried a big monkey wrench around the farm. In contrast to Ola who was short, stocky, sensible and hard working, Per was a tall and lanky dreamer.

The comic strip included Per's brother Lars. He was university educated, but absolutely useless on the farm. Having no idea how to harness a horse, he became the butt of community jokes. Polla, Ola's plump wife who came from Fargo, North Dakota, preferred city life and had no idea how to milk a cow. Her mother came out to the farm and turned out to be a real battle-axe.

These cartoons helped to popularize 'Norwegian stories." You can imagine the immigrants gathering in the small town cafe and roaring with laughter over such numbskull stories and riddles. After 1935, Rosendahl refused to draw any more cartoons and in 1942 he took his own life.

The "Ola og Per" comics used a slapstick approach to picture Norwegian-American life. They were in the style of "Mutt and Jeff," the "Katzenjammer Kids" and "Bringing Up Father." The Norwegian dialects come through in the cartoons.

A new volume entitled *Han Ola og han Per* (*He's Ole and he's Peter*) was printed both in Norwegian and in English. It contains the first 223 comic strips of the 599 that were published. Edited by Joan Buckley and Einar Haugen, it was published by the Norwegian-American Historical Association and the University Press in Oslo. One of the interesting features of the book is the vocabulary list at the bottom of each page. It's a good way to learn the folksy language of the immigrants, half filled with English.

These cartoons dealt with the struggles of immigrants in a strange land. The characters have both foibles and redeeming qualities. While many of the scenes were "violent," nobody ever got hurt. It's mostly reflexive humor, it turns back on the person who tries to be dramatic. We are indebted to the editors and publishers for making this fine volume available.

The people of Spring Grove still regard Rosendahl as one of their local heroes and a daughter-in-law, Georgia Rosendahl, is the local genealogist for the community.

CHAPTER 57

Who Are The 'Sons Of Norway?'

THE WINTER OF 1894-1895 was bleak in Minneapolis. It was a time of depression, unemployment and poverty. The Norwegians of North Minneapolis started to talk about what they could do to help their families and neighbors in the event of illness and death. Most of them had come from the areas of Trondheim and Selbu in Tronderlag. They met in Ingebret Rognaas' hardware store because, at age 40, he was more experienced than the other newcomers, having lived in America for 26 years. He was from Valdres.

They exchanged a lot of ideas and held an organizational meeting on January 16, 1895. At first they planned to call it the "Bjornstjerne Bjørnson Lodge," after the famous Norwegian writer. Deciding that this name was too difficult to say in English, they chose "Sonner af Norge" ("Sons of Norway"). All meetings were conducted in the Norwegian language. They voted in 1938 to change the official language of the organization to English and its monthly magazine changed in 1942. In 1896, they agreed to pay five dollars a week sick benefit to members and increased the funeral benefit to one hundred dollars.

We're indebted to Dr. Sverre Norborg, a native of Oslo, who has written a history of the Sons of Norway entitled *An American Saga*. He had been a professor at the University of Minnesota, Augsburg and Macalaster Colleges, as well as pastor in the Bergen Cathedral, Norwegian Seaman's Church in Brooklyn and of the Norwegian Memorial Church in Chicago (Logan Square).

The Sons of Norway was organized "To unite in a fraternal organization men and women of Norwegian birth, descent or affiliation, who are of good moral character." The term "affiliation" opens membership to anyone who happens to like a Norwegian.

Sons of Norway lodges are found in 29 states plus three Canadian provinces and even in Norway. The 110,000 members are divided into eight districts. Seven are in the United States and Canada and District

148

Eight is in Norway. North Dakota and Montana, plus Alberta and Saskatchewan comprise District 4. The International Headquarters are at 1455 West Lake Street, Minneapolis, MN 55408.

The *Viking* magazine published by the Sons of Norway always has a cover picture of Norway. The January 1987 issue had stories about the Leif Erikson Lodge in Ballard, Washington, about Bjorn Lasserud (a great skier), a story about the "Lyngen Horse," plus stories about food and news from the eight districts. After reading it for a while, one gets the feeling of knowing all these Norwegians. Many non-Norwegians join the organization (and hold offices too).

I joined the Sons of Norway in 1975, when planning our first trip to Norway. As you would expect, it's a group which is highly prejudiced about the goodness and importance of Norway. But it's also an open group, without prejudice towards other ethnic groups. They've gotten over the feelings of rivalry with Sweden. These were strong in 1905 when Norway separated from its sister nation and got its own royal family.

Travel and trade between the United States and Norway is important to this organization. The *Viking* magazine has advertisements for clogs and boots, heritage books, travel to Scandinavia, bunads, language study, festivals in Norway, auto rentals in Norway, dishes with rosemaling designs, a youth camp in Norway, art work and insurance, just to mention a few things. Sons of Norway members may visit Norway often, but there is no doubt about their loyalty to the New World. Patriotism has always been a part of their character.

Some people have wondered about the use of the word "lodge" in the organization, as it sometimes raises issues of conflict about religion. Theodore Graebner, writing in *A Handbook of Organizations* (Concordia Publishing House, 1948), stated that the Sons of Norway is not a secret society and has no altar, prayers or funeral ceremonies. He noted that political or religious issues are not allowed at meetings and that the "objects of the order are the preservation of Norwegian culture in America." He regarded it as a "nationalist society" and offered no objections to it.

One of the special projects promoted by Sons of Norway is "Ski For Light," a program which teaches blind people to ski. They also

149

underwrote a project for college students to travel across Greenland one summer. This had never been done before. Brave kids! It wasn't easy. Their latest big promotion is the "USA Cup," an annual soccer tournament at Blaine, Minnesota (the Twin Cities area). More than 400 young Norwegians attend the event, as well as youth from all over the United States and other foreign countries. Modelled after the Norway Cup in Oslo, it's the largest youth soccer tournament in America.

I was present at the dedication of "Skogfjorden," the Concordia College Norwegian Language Camp near Bemidji, Minnesota, over 20 years ago. The Sons of Norway was a major contributor to building this site. Our daughter, Lisa, and sons, John and Christopher, have attended the camp.

In June 1925, the Sons of Norway were involved in the Norse-American Centennial held at the Minnesota State Fair Grounds. Over 70,000 people were on hand as President Calvin Coolidge paid tribute to the Norwegian contributions to the United States. He said: "You have given your pledge to the Land of the Free. The pledge of the Norwegian people has never yet gone unredeemed." May it ever be so. We've come a long way since that cold day of January 1895 in our determination to be "united and true until Dovre falls" (a statement from the Constitution of 1814). The Dovre Mountains still stand.

Sons of Norway shield.

CHAPTER 58

The 'Bygdelag'
Movement In America

MORE THAN ANY PEOPLE I KNOW, the Norwegians loved to start ethnic organizations. In his book *A Folk Epic: The Bygdelag in America*, Prof. Odd Lovoll of St. Olaf College, lists 129 "bygdelags" (community lodges). Almost every section of Norway was organized in America according to their communities in the homeland.

I hold membership in the "Hallinglaget" which was organized at Walcott, North Dakota, on March 9, 1907. I was reared on a farm just seven miles south of Walcott. Their first "stevne" (convention) was held on May 17 of that year. Halling is my oldest heritage in America, dating from Hemsedal in 1867. My other heritages are from Numedal, Romsdal and Trøndelag. They also have organizations. My parents, however, did not join the local Hallinglag. I think that the reason is that the Hallings used to have dances and played cards. The piety of our home overruled such things. My home was also one of total abstinence from alcohol, tobacco, profanity and field work on Sundays. Good Friday was also kept as a day of rest and worship. I've never regretted this lifestyle.

The Hallings, like other clans of Norwegians, were organized in several local branches besides their national organization. The people of Gudbrandsdal had six "lags," one of which was organized in Minot, North Dakota, in 1930. Christian E. Lee was secretary of the Northwest Gudbrandsdalslag from 1938-1957. There were 15 Trønderlagets. The Northwest Valdreslag was organized in Minot in 1930. North Dakota Governor R. A. Nestos was president of the Vosselaget in 1924-1925.

As was typical of the "lag" minded Norwegians, they organized a national "Council of Bygdelags" in 1916. They were a powerful social force among the immigrants and their families. It's estimated that 75,000 people were involved in these organizations by the 1920s. In those early days, the bygdelags and the Sons of Norway were often rivals and even in opposition to each other. The one thing they all agreed with was the "Syttende Mai" (17th of May), the celebration of Norway's Constitution of 1814. There was a great deal of emotion and sentiment in the drive to start these "lags."

Most of these immigrants came from the rural areas of Norway. These new associations in America helped them to remember who they were and gave them courage to survive. The bygdelag provided "community" to these otherwise often shy newcomers. But in their "clan" meetings, these immigrants took courage in the new land. Many people planned for months to attend the next annual convention. They kept the old traditions alive. Songs, dances, fiddle playing, religious customs, dress styles and food have been preserved through these associations. The Norsk Høstfest is a social event that has brought Sons of Norway and bygdelag members together in one large celebration. A look at the variety of bunads (national dress costumes) at the Høstfest shows that the customs are still alive. And they still meet.

These rural folks represented the romantic aspirations of Norwegian ideals, as uninfluenced by life in the big cities and by the Danish rule from 1380 to 1814. With it was a return to the older way of speaking. This revival was called "Landsmaal" (the language of the land). One observer stated that "Norway is a country of many nations which naturally draw together when they get outside the country."

Even though the bygdelags grew up in the cities, it was mostly rural people who were their organizers. They'd advertise their meetings in the newspapers. People never seemed to grow weary of listening to speeches and the music of their homelands. It was an exercise in nostalgia of which they never tired. I suspect that some of those speeches got to be dull and drawn out, but it was the language and dialect of "home" and this was the most comforting sound that could come to their ears. Their hearts felt good. In every way, it was a grass roots movement that met the need of the people.

There was rivalry between the various bygdelags in the early days. One of the early leaders became so fanatical about the superiority of his group that it threatened the unity of Norwegians in America. My mother told me that this was often the case. If you weren't from a certain valley, you just didn't count for much among other Norwegians.

Unless you've been to Norway and seen the high mountain ranges and valleys, this might seem strange. Even today, despite national television and radio which tends to create uniformity in language, each valley of Norway has its own special way of talking, just like in the United States. Where I grew up, the Hallings and Trønders had difficulty understanding the Sognings. Since the Trønders came from the area of St. Olaf, they were especially sensitive to having "pure blood" among the Norwegians.

The bygdelags were found mostly in Minnesota, Wisconsin, northern Illinois, North and South Dakota. There were also a few in Canada and on the West Coast. There were none organized east of Chicago. Those were interesting days for the newcomers. It's easy to see why so many fellow countrymen settled in the Upper Midwest. There was always someone to welcome them and who would listen eagerly to their bragging about the Old Country which they had left behind.

CHAPTER 59

The Norwegian
Immigrant Press

ABOUT 400 NORWEGIAN LANGUAGE newspapers were started in America. Almost every immigrant family subscribed to one or more. What accounted for this eagerness to read? Strange as it may seem, the reason was a law made by the King of Denmark on Feb. 25, 1720, requiring public catechization of youth every Sunday between Easter and Michaelmas (Sept. 29). The strong emphasis on confirmation required that every young person could read. This made Denmark and Norway some of the most literate countries in the world.

Svein Nilsson (1826-1908) was an early Norwegian editor in America. He published *Billed Magazin* ("picture magazine") in Madison, Wisconsin, from 1868-1870. It was generations ahead of *Life* and *Look* magazines and sold for $1.00 a year or two cents an issue.

In 1870, Nilsson went to Chicago where he was editor-in-chief of the *Scandinavin* until 1886. *Scandinavin*, established in 1866, was a liberal Republican paper which became the most influential molder of opinion among Norwegian immigrants. Its sympathy was for the "common man" and it became a crusader for public schools. It opposed the Norwegian Lutheran Synod practice of establishing parochial schools.

It was in politics, however, that the Norwegian immigrant press found its focus. The immigrants held to their Democratic rural values and were surprised when America didn't turn out to be what the advertisements claimed. They had been duped by the travel agents who sold them tickets to a land where they could expect to get rich quick.

The early Norwegian settlers earned a reputation for being "independent." They preferred to live on farms where they could be their own bosses, rather than work in factories. The Yankee establishment was charged with caring more for their mules than their laborers, since mules cost money but workers were free. They started their newspapers as a voice of protest for social reform. Their ancient spirit of freedom would not die in the new land. Through their press, they attacked the Yankee philosophy of "rugged individualism" which grew rich on exploiting immigrants.

In North Dakota, the *Normanden* (1887-1954), published in Grand Forks, became the most influential Norwegian newspaper in the state. It began as an advocate for Populist views, but switched to being progressive Republican when the *Fram* in Fargo became the Norwegian voice of the Nonpartisan League. The Red River Valley was the center of the Norse immigrant press. Fargo had the most newspapers. Some of the other cities with influential newspapers were Enderlin, Portland and Hillsboro in North Dakota. Minneapolis and Fergus Falls in Minnesota, Sioux Falls, South Dakota, and Decorah, Iowa, were just a few of the other cities to have influential Norwegian newspapers.

The Norwegian and Yankee newspapers fought a continual battle over social issues. The Yankee writers charged that the unemployed were "tramps" and that the answer to poverty was to work harder. The Norwegians responded by accusing the bankers of greed. They urged Chicago meatpacker Jonathon Armour to set up a pension fund for his workers. While the Norwegians often disagreed with the labor union bosses who denied them jobs, they championed the cause of the labor movement. They claimed the answer was not "minimum wages," but "maximum wages" for a worker's toil. They challenged the employer to pay the worker the highest possible wages for work, not the least with which they could get away.

When the World War of 1914 came, the Norwegian press and congressmen stuck with the "neutralism" of their homeland and opposed President Wilson's pro-English policies. As a result, Norwegian-Americans were often charged with being "pro-German." This, unfortunately, happened to our family. Some Yankee school kids taunted my father as being "pro-German." A witness told me years later that this was the only time they had ever seen him angry. His oldest brother had been killed in France just a few weeks earlier. The Secret Service kept close watch on Dr. Markus Bøckman, president of Luther Theological Seminary in St. Paul, during the war years. A great biblical scholar, he lectured only in Norwegian. The government agents supposed that he was supporting the Kaiser's cause.

NORWEGIAN STORIES: IMMIGRATION PERIOD

Most Norwegian-American congressmen voted against Wilson's request for declaration of war on Germany. Senator Asle Gronna of North Dakota said, "I shall vote against war because I believe it would have been possible to maintain an honorable peace with all the nations of the earth . . . I am opposed to war because war means destruction, misery, and poverty to the toiling millions of our country for generations to come." A poll was taken in 1939 among Norwegian-Americans in which 105 out of 121 said they had opposed the war. Their common view held it to be a "money-man's war." I remember Dr. Iver Iverson, a history professor, tell us with a twinkle in his eye that America had been assured that we would not get into Europe's war because "the bankers won't allow it." The tables have now turned and the sons of the immigrants have become prominent bankers, but I can remember when the banker and the sheriff were feared among immigrant families, just as they had been in Norway.

Even though separated by a vast ocean from their homeland, the immigrants retained the humanitarian values of social justice learned in the old country. Their press was largely responsible for this. Today only two Norwegian language newspapers survive. They're located in Brooklyn and Seattle. But they belong to a proud heritage.

PART III

Norwegian Stories:
Norway and
Norwegians
Today

CHAPTER 60

King Olav V And
The Church Of Norway

H E WAS BORN JULY 2, 1903, in London, and baptized Aug. 11 with the name Alexander Edward Christian Frederick, after his English and Danish forefathers. From the day of his birth, he was destined to live no ordinary life. When he was just two — on Nov. 27, 1905 — his parents, Prince Carl of Denmark and Princess Maud of England, took up residence in Norway's royal palace as King Haakon VII and Queen Maud. Young Alexander, renamed Olav, was instantly loved by Norwegians everywhere.

The affection of the people of Norway for the young Crown Prince (now king) was shared by the Norse immigrant families around the world. His first trip to America, together with Crown Princess Martha (from the royal house of Sweden) in 1939, began a deep friendship that continues to the present day. The people of Minot still talk about his stop in this community. Following a state visit to Canada in 1987, His Majesty planned a trip as a private citizen to Norwegian-Americans in Minnesota and Iowa. On Nov. 27 (82 years to the day after he arrived in Norway), 1,300 people gathered in Minneapolis to honor him. The $37.50 per banquet ticket was no deterrent. My wife and I had invitations, but were not able to attend. It would have been a memorable event.

Much can be said about Norway's popular king. The one thing that has greatly impressed me about Olav V is his concern for the Church of Norway of which he is the head. If all the people of Norway shared the King's devotion to the Gospel, there wouldn't be standing room in the churches on any Sunday morning. He's a regular church-goer, wherever he happens to be. Even when he attends soccer games or is at a ski tournament, the King never misses Sunday worship.

How did this all begin? With the right parents, I suppose. His paternal grandmother, Queen Louise of Denmark, was a devout and highly talented Christian. She read every day to her children from the New Testament. She "had inherited the intelligence and spiritual vitality of

159

the Bernadottes," according to Sigurd Lunde, a contributor to a new book, *A King and His Church*, published in Oslo (1987). She also was affiliated with the inner mission circles in Copenhagen. This is typical of the piety found in the Danish royal family to this day. Olav's parents were also faithful worshippers and supporters of mission work. Among the guests in the Danish palace was Lars Skrefsrud, the renowned missionary to the Santals in India.

On our 1983 visit to Norway, my wife and I visited with Trygve S. Woxen, pastor of the Asker parish near the royal farm estate at Bygdøy, just west of Oslo. He often preached to the Royal Family and spoke highly of them to us. When the church was built, a separate entrance was provided for the King to enter. He advised the pastor, however, that when he attended Asker Church it would be through the regular doorway. He worships, sings hymns and takes communion as a regular participant with the congregation.

After the death of Haakon VII, Olav V was consecrated king at the Nidaros Cathedral in Trondheim on June 22, 1958 — exactly 52 years after his father's coronation. Olav chose to have a consecration service with prayers for his reign, rather than to wear the crown. At this service, the crown was placed at the foot of a silver crucifix atop the altar. He knelt before Trondheim's Bishop Arne Fjellbu (born in North Dakota) for the prayer: "Eternal God of power, bless our King; be his Lord and Sovereign always. And bestow every good gift upon his household in this life and in the life to come." Then they sang "A Mighty Fortress is our God." Bishop Johannes Smemo of Oslo preached the sermon, after which they sang "God save our gracious King."

In response to this moving ceremony, the King said "for my part it was no mere external formality. I can say with certainty that it was a sincere act." For over 30 years, Olav V has carried out his role as head of the church faithfully and effectively. Sadly, Olav's wife — Crown Princess Martha — died just a few days after their silver anniversary in 1954. (My good friend and former professor, Dr. Herman A. Preus, told me of attending her funeral.) As a result, Princess Astrid — Mrs. Johan Martin Ferner in private life — has often accompanied her father on state visits.

Besides visiting congregations in Norway, the King has taken a strong interest in Norwegian Seamen's Missions around the world. In 1982 he laid the cornerstone for the new Mission in Houston, and in 1983 he attended the 25th anniversary of the Mission in Kobe, Japan. He has also expressed appreciation and support for the work of the Lutheran Free Church as well as the Pentecostals, Salvation Army and other denominations in Norway. In 1967, on a trip to Rome, King Olav V paid a visit to Pope Paul VI at the Vatican.

One of King Olav's most interesting trips appears to have been his visit to Ethiopia in 1966. Emperor Haile Selassie personally met him at the airport in Addis Ababa and saluted him. A huge banner greeted him as they entered the city: "Welcome King Olav V! The Lord will keep your going out and your coming in!" quoting Psalm 121:8. The main purpose of the trip was to visit Norwegian mission stations in Ethiopia. The King had a special interest in the radio station RVOG ("Radio Voice of the Gospel") in Addis Ababa operated by the Lutheran World Federation, the most powerful station in Africa. When the pro-Soviet Socialist government overthrew Haile Selassie in 1974, it became a propaganda tool of the new military government.

Wherever he travels, whether in Norway or abroad, the King pays special attention to children. While in the Ethiopian capital, he opened the Norwegian School. He has also given strong support to relief work among the poor and hungry. When Princess Astrid visited nursing home residents while attending the Norsk Høstfest in 1983, she was doing what her father the King frequently does. Among the retirement homes the King has visited in America are Ebenezer in Minneapolis and Lyngblomsten in St. Paul. At Lyngblomsten, he met a man who had attended his father's coronation.

For the King's 75th birthday in 1978, the people of Norway raised 13 million kroner as a gift (about $2,500,000 at the time). He gave half of the amount to the Norwegian congregations in Copenhagen and Stockholm and the rest was put into a trust fund of which the interest of 10% goes to the Norwegian Seamen's Missions and a mission hospital in Irgalem, Ethiopia.

Wherever Norway's King goes, people meet him with great expressions of joy and gratitude for his presence. It's a sad commentary on the state of affairs in our country that heavy security is required when he comes to America. This is not the case in Norway and in most countries. When he visited Ethiopia, only two civilians attended him. One day in London, I'm told, a lady met him on the street and said: "You look just like King Olav!" He smiled and thanked her for the compliment.

The people of Norway are justly proud of their King, who so excellently embodies their highest values. We who are the children of immigrants from that land of the Midnight Sun share in this pride.

The consecration of King Olav V.

CHAPTER 61

The Prime Minister
Who Saved The King

AFTER WORLD WAR II, the Prime Minister of Norway, Carl J. Hambro, was welcomed to America as a hero of the Resistance. When he visited the Buck Ellingson farm near Hillsboro, North Dakota, the newspapers carried front page stories with a picture of him holding one of their children. It was touching. Hambro was regarded as next in importance to the king.

An air raid alarm went off in Oslo at 1:00 a.m. on April 9, 1940. Most people thought it was a routine drill, but Hambro, then President of the Storting (Parliament), immediately checked and found out that foreign men-of-war were steaming up the Oslofjord. He instantly understood the implications and advised King Haakon VII that the Royal Family and Storting members should take the next train to Hamar, 100 miles north. It was imperative that the King and his family should not fall into Nazi hands, as well as the royal gold reserves.

The Storting assembled and passed the necessary emergency legislation for the government to function outside of Oslo. Spies followed their every move. Barely had this been done when enemy war planes began to bomb their locations. They moved 20 miles east to Elverum, where at one point, both the King and Crown Prince Olav took shelter under a large tree during the bombing. If they had been killed, Prince Harald, just three years old, would have had a care-taker appointed for him by the Supreme Court. The Nazis planned to control that appointment and the country would be captive. Deep snow hampered travel through the mountains.

Back in Oslo, Vikdun Quisling, a former army officer, proclaimed himself "Chief of State" and appointed a "government" of virtually unknown people who were horrified when told of their new jobs. Quisling had just returned from seeing Hitler in Berlin two days earlier. Dr. Brauer, the German Minister in Norway, presented a list of demands between 4:30 and 5:00 a.m. which amounted to a complete surrender.

163

Delaying tactics were used before responding so the Royal Family would have time to travel further away from Oslo. The demands were then rejected.

After two months of heroic defense, the fighting was over in Norway and the government was relocated to London. Crown Princess Martha and her children, Ragnhild, Astrid and Harald, went to the USA where they were the personal guests of President and Mrs. Roosevelt at their Hyde Park home for the duration of the war.

Who was Carl J. Hambro? The Hambros had moved to Norway from England during the Swedish period (1814-1905) and became loyal citizens and significant servants of the nation. But there is an irony in the story. When the famous constitution of May 17 ("Syttende Mai"), 1814, was signed, it excluded Jews from Norway (also Jesuits). Only after this was changed in 1851, was it possible for the Hambros to become "Norwegians." The total number of Jews never exceeded 1500 before the war. But for this reason, Quisling and the Nazis had made a point of attacking Hambro. Throughout the war, he worked tirelessly for Norway's freedom as a leader for the government in exile.

It's a lucky thing that the original constitution was amended, or the Royal Family may have become hostage to Hitler on that fateful morning of April 9, 1940. Norway and Norwegians everywhere continue to honor the name of the Prime Minister who saved the King.

CHAPTER 62

The 'Resistance Museum' In Oslo

T HE SIGN AT THE ENTRANCE to Norway's Resistance Museum reads: "NEVER AGAIN." The Museum is located at Akershus Castle in Oslo's harbor. It was opened on May 8, 1970, by Crown Prince Harald, exactly 25 years after peace and constitutional government was restored. The purpose of the Museum is for "the young people of today and the coming generations."

It is still an embarrassment for Norway that it was so ill prepared to defend itself in 1940. But it's easy to understand. Norway had not been in a military conflict since 1814. The people trusted in their neutrality. None of its military leaders had been in a war. But 61 bitter months of occupation convinced its leaders that "never again" shall this happen. Despite its uneasiness about sharing a border with the Soviet Union, Norway is a cooperative member of NATO.

It was an unforgettable experience for my wife and myself to have been through the Museum, personally escorted by the Director, Reidar Thorpe. He had been a part of the Resistance. We learned that the last person he took through the Museum had been the US Secretary of Navy. He told us that the most important part of the Resistance was to help Norwegians to stand up against the Nazi propaganda to collaborate with the enemy. The Gestapo used both promises and cruelty to bend people's wills.

The name "Quisling" has come down in history as a term of shame. He was the leader of a small political party called "National Unity." It was Vikdun Quisling that urged Hitler to "save" Norway from the British and the Communists. Before the war, Quisling collected less than 2000 votes. At the end of the war, 40,000 had joined him, most of them quite innocently unaware of his Hitler connections. The underground newspapers led the cause for truth to the people. Dignity, calmness and discipline were the watchwords of Resistance leaders.

The Museum, called "Norges Hjemmefrontmuseum," is well researched and designed. Maps, secret papers, photos and audio-visuals bring the war years vividly to the visitor's awareness in 48 displays.

The saddest part was to see the torture tools used by the Gestapo. At the Grini Prison Camp near Oslo, 19,000 Norwegians were detained. 9000 more were sent to Germany, of whom 1340 died, including 610 Jewish Norwegians.

Germany and Norway have traditionally been friends, having bonds through church, commerce and culture. The well kept German cemeteries in Norway are a testimony to this. I visited one in Trondheim. It was heart rending to see the grave markers of so many youth who died for the follies of evil rulers.

A sign of the Resistance Movement was to wear a paper clip in a coat lapel. It means: "Let's Keep Together."

If you ever visit Oslo, be sure to visit the Resistance Museum. You will never forget it. Americans need to be reminded too that the price of freedom is "eternal vigilance." We all need to do our part so that this will "never again" happen in the lands we love.

CHAPTER **63**

Rjukan — Norway's Heavy
Water Plant Attacked

T HE DRIVE WEST FROM OSLO through Drammen, Kongs-
berg and Notodden is a delight to the eyes. As the mountains
grow more beautiful, the terrain becomes more rugged.
Thirty-five miles north is Rjukan ("Rookaan"), one of the
most important Allied targets during World War II.

On the evening of Feb. 27, 1943, nine Norwegians, led by Knut
Haukelid and trained in Great Britain by the SOE ("Special Operations
Executive"), climbed down a steep and icy mountainside, crossed a river
and climbed up another mountain to a heavily guarded factory which
produced "heavy water." They eluded the guards, broke into the factory,
poured out the water and planted explosives. They fled unseen. A
massive search by 3000 soldiers could not find them.

What was it all about? "Heavy water" or "deuterium oxide" looks and
tastes like other water, but it isn't. It was produced at the Norsk Hydro
plant under Nazi supervision for building atomic bombs for Hitler.
Rjukan was his only source of this rare liquid.

In 1939, Albert Einstein wrote to President Roosevelt that such a
weapon was possible. In June 1942, Churchill visited FDR. Rjukan was
heavy on his mind. He knew the danger if Hitler should get such a
weapon.

Four months later, a bomber took off from Scotland with highly
trained Norwegian saboteurs. The Hardanger Plateau below was an unfriendly place to drop by parachute. One of these young men was Knut
Haugland, an expert wireless operator. To see this peaceful looking man
today, you would never guess that he had been on that death defying
mission.

Rjukan is located in a valley only 300 yards wide. The defenses
seemed impregnable. However, a patriotic Norwegian scientist was in
charge of the plant. It was fortunate too that Prof. Leif Tronstad of
Trondheim had fled to England. He had designed the factory and was

able to build a mock-up of it so that the saboteurs knew their way around in it even if blindfolded. Microphotographs were smuggled in toothpaste tubes into Sweden and then to London.

The nine men who made the journey had suffered intensely for months on the cold, barren and windy plateau. Their food supplies had not lasted long enough. Reinforcements towed in gliders had perished. When they killed a reindeer, they ate "the whole thing."

By fall, the plant had been rebuilt and Hitler's timetable was back on schedule. A British air raid did little damage but killed 21 Norwegians. In February 1944, a large shipment of heavy water was ready to send to Germany. A ferry boat was to carry it over Lake Tinnsjo and out to sea. Saboteurs, led by Haukelid and dressed as workmen, planted explosives on board. At the deep end of the lake, an explosion rocked the belly of the ship. In four minutes it was gone. Hitler did not get his bomb.

The mountains around Rjukan are quiet today. But the valleys are alive with the memories of those days. If you ever visit Oslo, take a trip to Rjukan and see it for yourself. It's a part of the Scandinavian heritage.

CHAPTER 64

Knut Haukelid — Resistance Hero

THE STORY OF KNUT HAUKELID reads like a modern Scandinavian saga. Like so many Norwegians, his parents emigrated to America. When Knut and his twin sister, Sigrid Guri, were born, the parents went back to Norway. She became a movie actress. Their roots were at Rauland in Telemark. That's rugged mountain country.

This move was to be of critical importance to the whole free world. Knut, having the blood of Vikings, returned to America to study engineering. Then he studied in Germany. There his eyes were opened to the danger of war. He listened to Hitler's speeches and returned to Norway with disgust.

On April 9, 1940, when the Nazis attacked Norway, Knut was in Trondheim. He woke up in the morning to discover the city occupied by the enemy. Slipping into the countryside, he tried to join a fighting unit, but was unsuccessful. Norway had depended on its neutrality and was not ready for war.

Haukelid's day to serve his country came on February 28, 1943, when the British dropped him with nine other commandos on the Hardanger flats, some of the harshest winter terrain in the world. I have driven across it and have some idea of how difficult it would be to survive there in frozen snow. Stories have been written and movies have been made how they made their way by night to the Norsk Hydro Plant near Rjukan. Their mission was to destroy the plant which made heavy water (deuterium oxide). This substance would make it possible for Hitler's war machine to create a nuclear bomb. Eluding the guards, they destroyed both equipment and stores, and then escaped. The German occupation general, Nikolaus von Falkenhorst, said it was "the best coup I have ever seen."

The plant, however, was back in operation two months later. After the Americans bombed it in November, the Nazis decided to remove the equipment and heavy water stores to Germany. Informers within the plant sent word to Britain. Haukelid was given the task of preventing this transfer. Disguised as a laborer, he boarded the ship and planted 19 pounds of explosives. On Sunday morning, February 20, 1944, the ship carrying the dreaded cargo exploded and sank in the deepest part of Lake Tinnsjo. That ended Hitler's chance of getting the bomb.

The Resistance Museum in Oslo has an excellent exhibit of the hydro plant and how Haukelid and his companions did their work. If you go to Oslo, it is a "must" to see.

After the war, Haukelid became a Lt. Colonel and concentrated his energies on Norway's defense. Today, Knut and his wife, Bodil, spend their winters in Oslo and their summers at Lillesand, on the coast between Arendal and Kristiansand. He still finds time to go back to the family's mountain hotel at Rauland in northwest Telemark to hunt reindeer.

The Norsk Høstfest Association, honored Haukelid by inducting him into the Scandinavian-American Hall of Fame in 1985. It was a distinct privilege for my wife and I to be his hosts when he visited Minot. I also improved my knowledge of those dark days of World War II from our visits. Having dual citizenship in the United States and Norway, he brings honor to both countries for his dedication to freedom and peace. He has to be called one of the great heroes of the twentieth century.

CHAPTER 65

The Enigma Of
Vikdun Quisling

THERE ARE MANY WAYS to fame and remembrance, but few of us would like our name to be in the dictionaries as a by-word. Vikdun Abraham Lauritz Jonsson Quisling (1887-1945) has that distinction. The Merriam-Webster Dictionary refers to his name as someone who betrays his country and collaborates with the enemy.

Who was this man whose name is remembered with infamy by the whole world? It's not any easy story for a person of Norwegian heritage to tell. Vikdun Quisling was born in Fyresdal, Telemark, where his ancestors had provided the pastors for generations. They were also independent farmers and soldiers. His father, the rural dean of Lutheran clergy, was an eccentric intellectual, according to Paul M. Hayes, author of *Quisling: The Career and Political Ideas of Vikdun Quisling* (Indiana University Press, 1972). His mother also came from distinguished stock.

When Vikdun was 13, his father became pastor of the Gjerpen parish, near Skien. He had a brilliant academic record at the Skien high school, surpassing Henrik Ibsen, a distant relative. In 1905, he entered the Norwegian Military Academy and graduated with the highest records in the school's history. It was expected that he would have become either a pastor or a scientist. A bright future seemed assured.

Quisling, an apt student of languages, went to Russia, where Leon Trotsky offered to make him chief of staff in the Red Army in its war against the "Whites." He had also been invited to be an instructor for the Imperial Chinese Army. While turning down the Russian offer, he did spend many years there and became enamored of Communist ideology. Stalin's oppressive agricultural policies, however, changed his mind and he later became a bitter foe of Communism.

A fervent nationalist, Quisling's ambition was to be Norway's "savior" in a world that was becoming threatened with Communism and war.

This led him, as a disillusioned idealist, into the Nazi camp. Because of his aggressive and argumentative behavior, he alienated most of the people who might have helped him rise to prominence. In 1933, he organized the "Nasjonal Samling" ("National Unity") Party. Rejected at the polls, he started to negotiate with Hitler's aides and actually saw Der Fuehrer in Berlin on December 13, 1939. He urged a German invasion of Norway. His antagonists claim he was hoping to become the head of government in Oslo.

On April 9, 1940, "Operation Wilfed" was launched by the Nazis and Norway was occupied, but not without a struggle. The Nazis, however, didn't trust him or believe that he had a following among the people. It was assumed because of the neutralist position of the Norwegian government that the people would give no opposition. Even though they had not had a war for 116 years, nothing of the kind happened.

The war years were turbulent for Quisling and he made many trips to Germany to convince Hitler that he was their best bet for running the government. For the most part, he succeeded because the Nazi administration was so clumsy. In the early days of the invasion, Quisling made the Hotel Continental his headquarters. It's still an elegant hotel with excellent food service. I've stayed there a number of times. An attentive waitress "picked up" the list of cabinet members he was proposing and gave it to the Resistance. They went public with it. As a result, few were willing to accept the positions offered.

Still, Quisling succeeded in getting a large number of people to become dues paying members of his party. I've heard different figures ranging all the way from 40,000 to 70,000 and even more. His anti-Communist appeal lured many patriotic Norwegians to the Russian Front. A friend told me that her father volunteered so that his children "would not have to fight the Communists in Norway." After the war, her father was fined heavily and served a jail sentence. Knut Hamsun, the great novelist, also became an ardent National Unity Party member.

When the war ended, Quisling went to the Police Station on May 9, 1945, to negotiate a truce with the Resistance leaders. He was promptly arrested. After a highly publicized trial, he was found "guilty" and sentenced to death by a judge who had spent much of the war in a concentration camp. Quisling was executed at Akershus Castle about

2:30 a.m. on October 24, 1945. A gallery of distinguished sightseers was on hand to watch.

There is a bit of irony to his trial. Norway did not have a death penalty before the Nazi invasion. Quisling summed up the verdict himself when he said, "This case . . . is not just another judicial matter, but a question of politics." He was sentenced under a military law of 1902. His last days were spent reading the Bible and his father's writings, but he never "repented." Before his execution, he shook hands with the members of the firing squad. He is buried in the Gjerpen cemetery.

It's a mystery how this promising student should have chosen such a destructive way of life. I believe there are several reasons. Quisling took himself too seriously and felt that because of his superior intellect he alone was qualified to govern Norway. He also had come to love nature but distrust people. Imagine what he might have become if he would have had a sense of humor about himself.

CHAPTER 66

Thor Heyerdahl — Discoverer Of 'Old Worlds'

EW PEOPLE HAVE EXCITED THE WORLD with discoveries from past civilizations as Dr. Thor Heyerdahl of Norway. In 1947, he was thrust into international fame by his "Kon-Tiki" voyage. Heyerdahl wanted to test his theory that Polynesia "lay within the range of pre-European mariners from South America."

A thorough going scientist, Heyerdahl was convinced that the people of the Marquesas Islands of the South Pacific were related to the people of pre-Inca Peru. Rejecting popularly held theories that these islands could only have been reached from Asia, he built a balsa raft based on descriptions from early voyages. The wood was cut from the jungles of Ecuador. At the time, the experts said that it would never work. Balsa wood, they claimed, would become water-logged.

The Kon-Tiki sailed from Callao, Peru, on April 28, 1947. One hundred and one days later it ran aground on the coral atoll Raroia in Polynesia, 4300 miles from where it had begun. Heyerdahl never claimed that this proved history had happened in exactly that way but that it "could have happened."

There were days when the weather was too calm and when it was difficult to keep the raft in one piece. Swimming and fishing occupied a good deal of the crew's time. At one point, a 30-foot whale-shark followed directly underneath the raft. That was almost as long as the craft itself. At any time it could have upset the raft and plunged the crew of six to their deaths. This interfered with the daily swim and bathing of the sailors.

Fortunately for us, the Kon-Tiki has been preserved in a museum at Bygdøy Park in Oslo. I still remember my excitement when visiting it for the first time. I had read Heyerdahl's book in 1951. To see the preserved raft in near perfect condition was worth the trip overseas for me.

174

On a later trip to Norway, I visited with Knut Haugland, a member of the crew and now Director of the Kon-Tiki Museum. Haugland had first achieved fame as a member of the commando team that blew up the heavy water plan at Rjukan in February 1943. He was not at all the burly and tough looking person I had imagined, but rather a quiet mannered gentleman in a business suit who looks like any other Norwegian. I asked him about the Rjukan raid. He answered: "I've put that out of my mind and now like to remember the peacefulness of Polynesia." Later, however, he did discuss the raid with me. Among the things he mentioned was that in 1947 the oceans were clean. Then he showed me some chunks of crude oil found floating on the oceans in recent times and said that there is hardly any place where ocean water is unpolluted today.

Heyerdahl planned several more expeditions. These included the Galapagos Expedition of 1953, the Easter Island Expedition in 1955-1956, the Ra Expeditions of 1969-1970 from Morocco to Barbados and the Tigris Expedition from Iraq to Djibouti in East Africa in 1977-1978. The last one covered 4200 miles while greatly hampered by the troubled political times.

At the conclusion of the Tigris Expedition, the reed boat was ceremonially burned and an appeal was sent to the United Nations on behalf of peace. Heyerdahl is much more than a scientist. He is also a man with a political and social conscience, a trademark of Norwegian foreign policy today.

The Kon-Tiki Museum in Oslo contains many other items besides the raft from that first famous expedition. The pottery collection includes 131 jars of pre-Inca types. There is a model of the Easter Island stone giants and under the Kon-Tiki raft is a replica of the 30-foot whale-shark which bedevilled their journey. It's possible to walk underneath the raft in a life-like setting to see this fearful site through a window.

Heyerdahl is a master of many languages, including English and Polynesian. You would think that English was his native tongue when you read his books. His volume, *The Tigris Expedition*, shows him at his best. Aboard was an international crew of 11. They ranged in age from 20 to 63. From the United States came a contractor and a National Geographic cameraman. From the Soviet Union there was a carpenter and a physician who had attended astronauts. There was also crew from Germany, Mexico, Italy, Japan, Denmark, Norway and Iraq.

Heyerdahl now lives in Italy but frequently visits America and Norway. His latest book, *The Maldive Mystery*, was published in 1986. I had learned of it in a visit with Knut Haugland, but had no idea of the surprise awaiting me.

CHAPTER 67

Knut Hamsun —
Norway's Vagrant Novelist

SCANDINAVIA HAS PRODUCED MANY outstanding writers. The hardship of the land has caused much reflection on the meaning of life. One of these writers was Knut Hamsun (1859-1952), born on a small farm at Hameroy in Nordland, southwest of Narvik. Like so many of his countrymen, Hamsun visited America (1882-1884, 1886-1888). The New World, however, could not hold him. His first major writing, *Hunger*, revealed his critical feelings of North Dakota prairies and poverty in Oslo.

Hamsun's greatest novel was *Growth of the Soil* (1917). It's a glorification of the age old struggle to conquer the land and to make a living from it. A rugged individualist with no confidence in the masses or social programs for the poor, Hamsun struggled with faith and cynicism. His views were tainted by Nietzsche, a German philosopher who championed "nihilism."

Growth of the Soil won the Nobel prize for literature in 1920. Hamsun's reputation as a writer spread to both Germany and the English speaking world. The story took place in a northern region of Norway beyond civilization. Isak was a wonderer in search of good land without neighbors. He found his place and staked his claim. In the beginning, the only people he saw were occasional Lapps. He let it be known that he wanted a "woman-body" to come and help him. One came. Her name was Inger. She was no thing of beauty with her hair lip, but she was a hard worker and was good for Isak.

The story has tense drama. Isak never understood why Inger always got him out of the way when her babies came. It was only when a daughter was born with a hair lip, believed to be the black magic of the Lapps, that the reader sees into the dread of those mountain people. She strangled the child and eventually went to prison in Trondhjem for seven years where she learned many useful skills and had her hairlip repaired. To everyone's surprise, she became attractive and the envy of many neighbor women for her newly acquired sophistication.

A key person in the story is Geissler, a wondering businessman who took a liking to Isak and Inger and helped them to become the wealthiest family in the valley. Copper mining became the "get rich quick" hope of the community, but it didn't last. The people would have been better off sticking to their farming. Isak's two sons were symbolic of the youth of Norway in those days. The younger, Sivert, became a good farmer and stayed with his father. The older, Eleseus, had big ideas but failed at everything. Finally, he emigrated to America. It was commonly held that if people couldn't be successful in Norway, they could always go to the New World. My wife's mother tells us that this is also what people in Denmark used to say.

After gaining fame, Hamsun settled down in southern Norway as a gentleman farmer. In 1984, travelling between Skien and Kristiansand, I saw the farm. It touched off a lot of thoughts.

During World War II, Hamsun supported Quisling's National Unity Party for which he was fined 325,000 kroner after the war. Many Norwegians, however, have forgiven him for his war time political views and continue to honor him as a writer. Alexander Solzhenitsyn quoted Hamsun in his novel, *August 1914*, as saying "The Slavs are a turbulent people and will be the conquerors of the world after the Germans." This may explain his pro-Hitler views. There were other Norwegian idealists who also chose Hitler as a way of stemming the Slavic tide of Russian Communism.

H. G. Wells admired *Growth of the Soil* and wrote: "The book impresses me as among the very greatest novels I have ever read. It is wholly beautiful; it is saturated with wisdom and humor and tenderness." Enigma that Hamsun was, I agree and highly recommend it.

Hans Hyldbakk —
'King Of The Cliff'

"**K**LEIVAKONGEN," "KING OF THE CLIFF," they call him. Hans Hyldbakk is the best known person in Surnadal, my ancestral valley, 75 miles southwest of Trondheim. At 88, he was waiting for another book of poems to be published. In addition to poetry, Hyldbakk has published seven large volumes of local history called "bygdeboker."

My visit to this famous writer in September 1985 was a moment of excitement. He is the only living link between our family before the immigration and myself. After grandpa Ola (Ole) Olsen Fiske emigrated to America in 1892, great-grandmother Margrethe was left alone with her small herd of cattle and goats. During the summer, she assumed the role of a dairymaid and went up to the Fiske seter (summer pasture) in the Trollheim mountains.

In 1910, when Hans was 13, he was a "gjaetar" (literally, "goatherd") in that seter. He wrote a poem about Margrethe, describing her as the best of the dairymaids. When she served the boys cream for their bread, she dipped deep into the container to bring up the thickest and sweetest. She also darned their socks, dried their wet clothes and made their beds. They didn't forget. Margrethe lived until 1920 and never saw grandpa Ole after he emigrated to North Dakota. I just discovered this good woman a few years ago, but now her picture hangs proudly in our family room.

Hyldbakk lives in a small hytte (cottage) high above the village. To get there we had to drive through cattle gates over a switchback trail. Directing us to his home was a local journalist, Magne Holten. It was a beautifully cool morning with bright sunshine. I could see why Hans liked it up there. He had a telephone, but neither radio nor television. As we sat across the table from each other, I felt an instant comraderie with this spry and modest man who had researched the records and traced my roots back to 1520.

A few years ago, another Surnadal journalist led a movement to get the University of Oslo to give Hyldbakk an honorary doctor's degree. When learning of it, he made it clear that the degree would be refused. Instead, a bust of Hyldbakk was placed near the courthouse. I had my picture taken by it.

A couple of weeks after returning home, a newspaper arrived from Surnadal. There was a full page story by Holten about our visit. The headline read, "Prest med røter fra Fiske pa Surnadals-visit." (Priest with roots from Fiske on a Surnadal visit.) There was a picture of Hyldbakk standing between my wife and myself. Holten made a point of writing that my wife is "of Danish blood." Another writer advised me that Norwegians consider a man fortunate if he has a Danish wife. That makes me a success in Surnadal! To top off the trip, Hyldbakk identified some previously unknown relatives.

When taking leave of this delightful gentleman, I promised to write a story about him. He replied with a smile, "Then I'll be famous in America." Long may he live and probably will from climbing that mountain. I agree, he is the "King of the Cliff."

CHAPTER 69

Sigrid Undset —
Norwegian Nobel Laureate

THE FIRST TIME I ENCOUNTERED the writings of Sigrid Undset (1882-1949) was in 1940 as a freshman in the Colfax High School library in southeastern North Dakota. It was a very modest library, to say the least, hardly more than a few bookcases, but it provided some excellent reading.

I checked out Undset's *The Bridal Wreath*, part of the "Kristin Lavransdatter" trilogy set in 14th-century Norway in the mountainous area near Trondheim. Since our school was in a predominantly Norwegian ethnic community, it's not surprising that its library contained this famous trilogy. Another major work of Undset's is *The Master of Hestviken*, a series of four related novels set in 13th century Norway.

Sigrid Undset was born in Kallundborg, Denmark, the oldest daughter in a family of three sisters. Her father was a famous Norwegian archaeologist who kindled her interest in Norway's medieval history. Her first novel was set in the Middle Ages, but the publisher rejected it and urged her to switch to modern topics. She tried it for a while and then returned to her favorite theme, explaining, "the human heart does not change in the least through all the ages." The subjects which run through her writings are love, sexuality and our accountability to God and to other people. Her writings involve struggle betweeen the realistic and the ethical. That's not an easy task.

Fame came to Undset in 1911 through her novel *Jenny*. Norwegian television has produced this story about the struggle for women's liberation, with Liv Ullmann playing the lead. The story is set primarily in Rome, where Jenny went to become an artist. She had the talent but failed because her emotions got in the way of her work. The book caused a sensation because of Undset's frankness in expressing women's feelings.

A niece of Undset's, Charlotte Blindheim, wrote of the famous author in the *Scandinavian Review* (1982). There was an aura of respect and awe for this celebrated aunt whom she calls "Moster" (mother's sister) Sigrid. It's a term of respect, affection and closeness that my wife's mother has often used of her family in Denmark. In a "moster" relationship, cousins feel almost as close as brothers and sisters.

Sigrid was married in 1912 to Anders Svarstad. They had three children, two sons and a daughter. The daughter was mentally retarded and the oldest son, Anders, was killed during the invasion of Norway in 1940. She never got over the sorrow of her son's death.

Undset's great fame came in 1928 when she was awarded the Nobel prize for literature. When the Nazis invaded Norway, she fled to the United States for the duration of the war. While in America, Undset supported Norway's war effort by writing novels for the Norwegian Information Service. She also wrote an essay about a childhood friend who was shot down over Normandy in 1943. After the war, Undset returned to her own house in Lillehammer, called Bjerkebaek, where she died in 1949.

Bjerkebaek, completed in 1924, was a substantial house — one might even call it a villa. Her niece writes that "every object was stamped with Moster Sigrid's highly personal taste, every room marked by her sure sense of each thing's own beauty." She especially remembered the 12 Christmas Eves that she and her sisters spent at Bjerkebaek.

Undset had a great love for botany and her house was always well furnished with plants and flowers. Her son, Hans, wrote of this love: "Her relationship with flowers came to be legendary even in her own lifetime. She got around plants. She communicated with them. And I don't insult either her or you when I say that as difficult as her association with people could be on occasion — just as undifficult was her association with flowers. It wasn't feigned. They didn't ask stupid questions. In a word, they didn't bother her." That tells us a lot about this great author. During the war years, she travelled to New England from her residence in New York City to study flora.

Bjerkebaek was never the same after the war. The Germans had occupied the house for three years and Undset had lost two of her children. She never wrote another novel. Peter Egge, a long-time friend wrote of her: "She was solitary as a genius always is, despite friends and world renown. She lived a life of inner struggle, accompanied by unspoken, defeating fears and secret glorious victories. The struggle was a precondition of her genius."

Undset liked to read to children, especially from the Sagas and English lyric poetry. She also came to enjoy Shelley, the Bronte sisters, Emily Dickinson and Willa Cather. Reading to children is, in my opinion, a virtue worthy of note.

It was no minor scandal in Norway when, in 1924, Undset decided to become a Roman Catholic. From then on, she wrote from her new point of view. Having been raised in a "lukewarm" Lutheranism, she seems to have been drawn to pre-Reformation Norway through her studies and writings of the Middle Ages. The following year, Undset divorced her husband and never remarried. She also broke with the liberal and feminist company of her youth.

A few years ago, a Benedictine Brother at St. John's Abbey in Collegeville, Minnesota, corresponded with me about Sigrid Undset, stating that he wished to visit her grave to pray there. My wife and I have an author friend in Norway who, like Undset, converted to Roman Catholicism. I told her that this made her a "Protestant" since she was protesting against the State Church. After some thought, she accepted the epithet.

Sigrid Undset was a remarkable person as well as a famous writer. I get the feeling when reading *Kristin Lavransdatter* that she was writing about herself, but transplanted back 600 years in time. Her father died when she was 11 and this put the family into difficulty. For 10 years, 1899-1909, she supported them by working as a clerk by day and writing by night. With the publication of *Jenny* in 1911, she no longer needed the clerking job.

Anyone who wants to know about Norway in the Middle Ages can hardly do better than to read Undset's novels. It takes patience, however, because they are long and require a lot of deep thought. The historical setting may also be unfamiliar, but for those who stick with it, the rewards are great. We who claim the Norse heritage are all in her debt.

CHAPTER 70

Alfred Nobel
And The 'Prizes'

IF YOU TAKE A TOUR of Stockholm, your guide will certainly point out the Grand Hotel and comment, "That's where the Nobel prizes are announced." The awards in physics, chemistry, medicine and literature have been given there since 1901. The award for economics, given only since 1969, is also announced in Stockholm. The politically important Nobel Peace Prize is given out in Oslo.

The man who started the world's most prestigious awards was Alfred Nobel (1833-1896), a Swedish chemist. Nobel's father had been an inventor and made it possible for him to study in St. Petersburg (Leningrad) and in the United States. His international fame came from experimenting with nitroglycerin in his father's factory. In 1867, after years of work, he combined it with an absorbent substance that could be safely shipped. He called it "dynamite," from a Greek word meaning "power." Nobel intended it to be used for peaceful purposes, especially in engineering and in road building.

It wasn't long before Nobel became one of the richest men in the world. He built factories in many countries and purchased the Bofors armament plant in Sweden. Among the other things he experimented on were synthetic rubber and artificial silk. A lover of literature, he wrote several plays and novels. These, however, did not bring him fame.

An idealistic Swede, Nobel's fragile health suffered intense guilt when he saw his prized dynamite being used for war. He had only thought of peace. In his will, an endowment fund of $9,000,000, money from his estate, was set aside for prizes to promote international peace. The value of each prize had reached $180,000 by 1981. The Swedish Central Bank provides the money for the economics prize.

All the awards, except the Peace Prize, are given out in Stockholm. But for some unclear reason, Nobel turned over the management of this award to the Norwegian Parliament (Storting) which appoints a committee of five to make its selection. All the awards are made on

December 10, the anniversary of Nobel's death. Two or more persons may share the prize, or no award may be made at all. No one is allowed to apply for these prizes. Nominations must be made by a "qualified" person.

Immense prestige is connected with the Nobel prizes in addition to the money. I noted this on a trip to Norway in 1985 when I obtained a copy of the Yearbook for the Norwegian (State) Church. The picture of Bishop Desmond Tutu of South Africa was on the front cover. In the American press, hardly a reference is made to the Bishop without noting that he is a "Nobel Peace Prize" winner. The award reflects the feelings of the Norwegian people. They are among the strongest to oppose the Apartheid policies of the South African government. The Scandinavian Air System has stopped flights to South Africa. This recognition of Bishop Tuto has added to his stature as a leader in his country.

To read through the list of awards since they began in 1901 is to review a "who's who" of the world's most influential people in the 20th century. Besides Bishop Tuto, some of the other award winners have been Wilhelm Roentgen, Theodore Roosevelt, Rudyard Kippling, Albert Einstein, Selma Lagerlof, George Bernard Shaw, Niels Bohr, Arthur Compton, Jane Addams, Enrico Fermi, Linus Pauling, Winston Churchill, Dag Hammarskjold, Albert Schweitzer, Milton Friedman, Norman Borlaug, Elli Wiesel and Mother Theresa. Americans have won the largest number of awards, followed by the Germans, English and French. Seven organizations have won awards, including the United Nations High Commission of Refugees. Only two winners have declined to accept, Boris Pasternak (1973) and Jean Paul Sartre (1977), both in literature.

It's a strange twist of events that the Scandinavians, once the terror of western Europe, should now be the world's foremost promoters of peace; and that the invention of dynamite, intended for peace, should now be the stock in trade for terrorists. The $9,000,000 trust fund still speaks eloquently in a time when the money of "influence" is counted rather in the billions.

CHAPTER 71

Carl Ben Eielson —
'Viking In The Sky'

THEY CALLED HIM BEN, but he was a "Viking in the Sky." Carl Benjamin Eielson was born July 20, 1897, in Hatton, one of North Dakota's most solid Scandinavian communities.

Ben's father operated a family store in which the future Arctic hero often clerked. Those country stores sold everything a family needed: groceries, clothing, hardware, toys and even salt blocks for the livestock. They also bought eggs and cream from the farmers. But Ben's heart wasn't in the store. It was in the out of doors where he could hunt, swim and go hiking in the woods. In school, Ben was a true scholar and he excelled in debating and sports.

After high school, Ben went off to study law, first at the University of North Dakota in nearby Grand Forks, and later at the University of Wisconsin. In 1929, both schools selected him as one of their most famous alumni. While at Wisconsin, he enlisted in the air service of the US Army on Jan. 17, 1917. After completing his training, he became a Second Lieutenant (later he beame a Colonel). But the war ended and instead of going to France, he went back to Hatton. There he did more clerking and helped to organize an American Legion post.

Flying became Ben's passion. He organized a flying club and went into a partnership to buy a single engine Curtis plane for $2585. He had found his love—stunt flying and giving rides at county fairs. It went pretty well until he hit an air pocket and the plane lost a wing to a telephone line.

Having received his university degree, Ben enrolled at Georgetown University in Washington, D.C., to become serious about law again. People growing up today may not see anything so unusual about this, but back in the 1920s this was not typical. Most North Dakotans at that time did not even get a high school diploma, not to mention a college degree or attend graduate school.

While in Washington, Ben met a congressman from Alaska who offered him a job as high school principal in Fairbanks. No sooner was he there than he took to flying again. The Yukon Indians were so amazed at Ben that they called him a "Moose Ptarmigan," a grouse with feathered feet that habitated on a moose. On Feb. 21, 1924, Ben made history by flying 500 pounds of mail over 300 miles. It took about five hours instead of the usual month by dog sled. Ben also developed a new type of ski for heavy planes.

Ben was a "pro" and in demand by the best in the business. Wilhjalmur Steffanson, a famous Icelandic-American explorer of the polar regions, wanted Ben to work for him. On one such trip, he was forced down on an ice flow and had to walk over 100 miles to safety. It took 18 days. He was also the first to fly over the North Pole.

In 1928, Ben was an international hero and was honored wherever he travelled. He had not forgotten Hatton, however, and his hometown friends had not forgotten him. On July 21, 1928, they gave him one of the biggest welcomes ever held in the state.

Ben was born for flying and there was no stopping him now. He also made aviation history in Antarctica, covering over 1200 miles that had not been previously mapped.

Then came the final flight. A ship was frozen off the coast of Siberia. Ben and his mechanic, Earl Borland, responded. One rescue attempt was successful. A second was never completed. Ben was lost on Nov. 9, 1929, in a storm. It was suspected that the altimeter was defective. It took over two and a half months to find the wreckage. On March 24, 1930, Hatton and the whole state paid tribute to Ben in the largest funeral in North Dakota's history. Over 10,000 people crowded into the little city. Memorial services were held in other cities too. Schools closed as all eyes focused on St. John's Lutheran Church where the family held membership.

Is Ben forgotten? Not in Hatton. His childhood home has now become a Registered Landmark Historical Site and museum to honor him. It's an impressive building on the outside and the inside reveals woodworking craftsmanship that's difficult to find today. Pictures of Ben and other memorabilia reveal the high estimate in which this young Halling was held by famous people of his day.

Ben is also remembered at the state's Heritage Museum in Bismarck. His artifacts have been displayed at the Norsk Høstfest in Minot and Ben was inducted into the Høstfest's Scandinavian-American Hall of Fame in 1984. He is also remembered in Alaska at the Strategic Air Command's Eielson Air Force Base and by Mt. Eielson, near Mt. McKinley.

There will be more honors for Ben. Heroes like this "Viking in the Sky" will never die in the memories of people whose ethnic pride is just beginning to bloom.

Carl Ben Eielson.

CHAPTER 72

T. F. Gullixson — As I Remember Him

I FIRST HEARD HIS ELOQUENT VOICE in the spring of 1944. His theme, "We Live To Bequeath," still rings in my memory. The words were a manifesto of the life he lived. Thaddaeus Francke Gullixson was born Sept. 4, 1882, on a homestead in the Des Moines River Valley near Bode, Iowa.

His early days on the farm taught him the love of land and the sacredness of community. It also imbedded in his soul the value of hard work and the awareness of human frailty. In one of his books, he tells the story of driving a team of runaway horses pulling an empty hayrack and how his father's strong arms and voice brought the team to a halt. In the years to come, he saw his father's hands as the hands of God.

"Tad," as they called him, was needed on the farm as older brother, George, was ordained into the ministry when Tad was only 11. But Tad was to follow. He attended Bruflat Academy in Portland, North Dakota, and then went on to Luther College in Decorah, Iowa. After completing theological studies at Luther Seminary in St. Paul, Minnesota, he spent the academic year 1906-1907 at Johns Hopkins University in Baltimore. It promised to be a brilliant career in Old Testament studies. He mentioned his graduate studies to me on a couple of occasions. Each time a "light" came into his aging eyes. But then came a Letter of Call from a "West River" congregation in Pierre, South Dakota.

In 1911, after four years of ministering to cowboys on the frontier, he became the pastor of First Lutheran Church in Minot, North Dakota, where he remained until 1930. His mark on the community is still keenly felt by the many who knew him. His concern for the community has been memorialized by Trinity Medical Center of which he was a founder and board chairman. One of his cherished friends in Minot was Ragnvald Nestos, who was governor of North Dakota from 1921-1925.

For 25 years, from 1930-1955, Gullixson was president of Luther Theological Seminary in St. Paul and at the same time was vice-president of the former Norwegian Lutheran Church in America, later named Evangelical Lutheran Church. My closest contact with "Dr. Gullixson," as we students always called him, was from 1948-1954. When I graduated from seminary in 1952, it was his encouragement that brought me back to the campus to earn an advanced degree in 1956.

His personal life and views were never the primary subject of his lectures, conversations or sermons. But these things did drop here and there and they were gathered as precious gems by those of us who were in his presence. O. G. Malmin, former editor of the *Lutheran Herald*, described Gullixson's preaching as "biblical, confessional and contemporary." I would add the word "doxological" or the "praise of God" to this list.

Gullixson had a keen musical ability. While pastor in Minot, he was also choir director. He was on the editorial board of the popular hymnal called the *Concordia*. He was also a member of the Joint Union Committee which guided the formation of the American Lutheran Church in 1960.

The eminent seminary president was like a "father" to many of us who received our professional education under his influence. While he could be uncompromising in the presence of his peers, he never forgot what it was like to be a boy. Toughness and gentleness were close together in his spirit. In the fall of 1949, he spoke in chapel for a week on the theme "No Minimums" in scholarship, humility, faithfulness, courage and patience. His words had a way of taking deep root in the listener's soul. I can still hear that voice with its majestic cadence and vibrato. We considered ourselves fortunate if he would ever invite us into his office just to chat. We valued every moment of it.

When he died on April 2, 1969, an era ended for many of us. Just five days later on April 7, Easter Monday, another era ended for me. My own father died. I had lost two "fathers" in one week. "We live to bequeath" was a fitting epitaph for both of them.

CHAPTER 73

Myron Floren
Goes To Norway

THE HEART LONGS TO GO HOME. It was so for Myron Floren, the best known accordionist in America. "Home," in this case was not Webster, South Dakota, where he began life, nor in Rolling Hills, California, where he lives with his family, but Norway, the land of his roots.

Floren has become a favorite with people who attend the Norsk Høstfest in Minot, North Dakota. People return every year from all over the United States and Canada to hear him again. They stand to applaud even before he begins to play the old time polkas, schottishes, waltzes and gospel songs.

The Høstfest sponsored a Norway trip featuring Floren in the summer of 1985. It was conducted by Carrol T. Juven of Fargo, North Dakota, a veteran traveler of more than 50 trips to Norway and whose roots are in Hallingdal. Accompanying the famous accordionist was the "Joe Alme Big Band" ("Stor Band" in Norwegian). Prof. Joseph Alme, Director of the International Music Camp at the Peace Gardens bordering North Dakota and Manitoba, is a popular and respected musician in the Midwest. Many of Floren's friends were along on the tour.

The tour began in Oslo and then travelled over the Haukeli Mountains to Bergen. There they enjoyed a visit with His Honor, Haakon Randal, Governor of Hordaland. They had met two years before at the Høstfest. My wife and I visited Governor Randal a few weeks later in Bergen. He was still excited to have had Floren perform in his capital city.

From Bergen they travelled over the mountain roads and fjords to Skei where they joined in an evening of musical fun with the "Fjellklang Spelemannslag," a group of local entertainers whom Floren had met previously at the Høstfest. From there they travelled across the Geiranger Fjord, down the steep and winding Trollstig Road to Aandalsness. Then they crossed over more mountains and fjords to Trondheim, where Floren traces some of his ancestry. In Trondheim, a woman who had seen him perform in America, came on stage during the concert with a big bouquet of roses to present to the famed accordionist, much to the pleasure of the audience.

No trip connected with the Høstfest would be complete without stopping at Skien, Minot's "Sister City." This visit was special because it coincided with the Telemark "Handelstevnet" (Trade Fair). They toured the Porsgrunn Porcelain Factory and visited with its owner, Kjell Strand, who has attended the Høstfest many times.

Floren's popularity in Norway was enhanced by his ability to speak Norwegian. This always surprises our cousins across the sea, especially if we happen to speak with one of the local dialects.

Alme said, "I found our trip to Norway to be both exciting and refreshing." "Exciting" because Floren is an outstanding professional and "refreshing" because of Norway's beautiful scenery and the hospitality of its people. Alme, like others on the tour, contacted relatives that they did not know existed. He commented, "travelling and performing with Myron Floren in Norway was one of the greatest experiences one can ever have."

Alme's band members are themselves all outstanding musicians. Every member had to be able to play two or more instruments. Besides Alme from North Dakota, they included Cordell Bugbee, Harlan Helgeson and Robert Quebbemann of Minot; Scott Greenwood of Westhope; Gordon Lindquist of Bottineau; Orville Roble of Harvey; and Guy Shobe of Stanley; Jim Beer and Ed Mantuefel of Winnipeg, Manitoba were also part of the "Big Band."

Receptions were held for Floren and his entourage wherever they visited and press coverage was lavish with praise. The people were captivated with his charming personality and excellent musicianship. They're already waiting for his next "homecoming." Floren hasn't announced when he'll make his next trip to Norway, but he's promised to keep coming back to the Høstfest. They are his most enthusiastic audience anywhere. We hope that will be a long time.

CHAPTER 74

Erling Rolfsrud And
The 'Tiger-Lily Years'

I FIRST MET ERLING NIKOLAI ROLFSRUD in the fall of 1944 when I was a freshman at Concordia College in Moorhead, Minnesota. He was Chairman of the Department of Business Education and I was a half-scared boy that barely got off the tractor in time to start school. I never took any business classes from him, but I always felt that he liked me. This was reassuring to the country boy who was reared with immigrant values.

Rolfsrud left Concordia after that year and I can't remember meeting him again until the 1986 Norsk Høstfest. During these years, he became one of the best known writers in the Midwest. We read his books to our children. *Gopher Tails for Papa* (1951) and *Boy from Johnny Butte* (1956) were part of their growing up.

His book, *Scandinavian Moses* (1986) brought him to Minot for the Høstfest. It's the story of Knute Nelson, an immigrant boy from Norway, who was as important in politics to Norwegian Americans as Martin Luther King was to Black Americans. His success broke the barrier that had kept the Norsk immigrants in "bondage." From 1882 until his death in 1923, Nelson was a Congressman, Governor and Senator from Minnesota. Rolfsrud returned to the Høstfest in 1987 with *Notable North Dakotans*, which includes several stories on Scandinavians.

Having done an article on Nelson in the *Scandinavian Heritage*, I asked Rolfsrud how he happened to write a book about this "grand old man of Minnesota." I should have known. Rolfsrud's home is near Alexandria where Nelson had lived. He'd been involved in saving the Nelson house as an historical building.

Rolfsrud has written 26 books on a wide range of subjects since his *Lanterns Over the Prairies* in 1949. After the Høstfest, I called him and said I'd like to do a story on him. He kindly consented to share some anecdotal material. I especially asked for information about his boyhood. He sent me his book, *The Tiger-Lily Years* (1975), which was written for his children and grandchildren to tell them what life was like before "supersonic transportation, shopping malls, plastic flowers, and quick food stops." It describes his growing up on a farm near Keene, North Dakota, and attending a country grade school in the far western part of the state.

This man who has become one of the outstanding Midwest writers was sent out to pick tiger lilies for his father's funeral. The book is his "confession" about the meaning of life learned in the aftermath of those days. While his older brother Halvor took over the man's work on the farm at age 14, Erling discovered that he liked to do the things that were teasing material for other boys. He enjoyed flowers, playing the organ and books. Of course, he also liked it when Halvor let him drive the horses to town with a load of grain or the tractor for plowing. Halvor went on to be a successful farmer and a highly regarded state legislator. It was to his immigrant mother, however, that Rolfsrud pays the highest tributes. She inspired the desire in him for an education.

I always like to find out about the child that precedes the adult. Children are, I believe, the most exciting people in the world. Having read *The Tiger-Lily Years*, I now understand why Erling Rolfsrud is still the delightful person I'd known him to be. He discovered that the Yankee neighbors hugged and kissed their children. In the Rolfsrud home, like in so many Norwegian homes, children were expected to know that their parents loved them without a display of affection. Affection would "spoil" them. Rolfsrud liked the Yankee ways better.

Rolfsrud's memory has phenomenal recall. He gives minute details about the cost of a mackinaw from Sears & Roebuck ($5.45), details on cars which the neighbors drove, the description of his new suit with longs pants for eighth grade graduation and gathering 17 sacks of cow chips as a birthday present for his mother.

Besides writing books, Rolfsrud also has a weekly syndicated column which appears in newspapers throughout North Dakota and Minnesota. As expected, they're excellently written and fascinating to read. He writes on a wide variety of subjects. The one which has interested me most was his reflections on "hardships" while a college student in the early 1930s. He relates how he taught in a one-room grade school in 1930 for $81 per month. To qualify for the job, he borrowed $120 from a bank to attend summer school at the Minot State Teacher's College. Staying in the schoolhouse, he walked 14 miles home for the weekends when his brother could not come and get him. After three years of teaching, despite reducing salaries due to the Depression, he saved enough to finance one year at Concordia College. He washed a lot of dishes for his college degree which was earned in three years.

All through his life, the church has been important to Rolfsrud. Besides writing articles for Sunday school papers, he has been a church organist for 30 years.

We compared some notes about writing and I was not surpised to learn that he has that inner compulsion of necessity which drives many of us to write. For two years, he was Associate Editor of *The North Dakota Teacher* and also lectured in 175 schools across the state. It was fitting that Erling Rolfsrud was selected as one of the 75 "heroes" of North Dakota in 1964 for the state's Diamond Jubilee. Those "Tiger-Lily Years" have blossomed. I hope he brings another new book to the Høstfest next year.

CHAPTER 75

George Reishus
Remembers

THERE IS NOTHING SO EXCITING as seeing the world through the eyes of a child. One of the great losses to the world is that so much history is written by people who have forgotten their childhood perspectives. This was not the case with George Alfred Reishus (1886-1972), whose Norwegian family moved from Minnesota to Minot, North Dakota, in 1887 when the "Magic City" was just beginning. It was cowboy country in those days and Reishus has left us a vivid description of it in his book *Gone Are the Days*, published in 1954.

The Reishus family was among the earliest of Norwegian families to settle in the Midwest. George's uncle, Torjus, who came to Minot in 1886 to become pastor of First Lutheran Church, was born at Koshkonong, Wisconsin, in 1847. This is one of the historic Norse settlements in America. George was an uncle to my long time friend, Dr. Roy Harrisville, professor at Luther Northwestern Theological Seminary in St. Paul, Minnesota. So I find his recollections doubly interesting.

His early remembrance of Minot was as a city of cowboys, gunslingers, Indians, hunters, trappers, gamblers, construction crews, fistfights, scouts, "fancy girls," merchants and farmers. He recalled that there were were two places he was forbidden to go near. One was the row of houses near the railroad tracks where the "fancy girls" lived with their red lamps burning night and day. The other was the coulees in the southwest part of the town because the Indians encamped on what we now know as "South Hill," where I've lived for 14 years. He told the story how his new cap was swished from his head one day when he ventured too close to the forbidden coulees. It took a trip with his father to the teepees to recover it.

He remembered the courage of the frontier women. His own mother, Astrid, known for her gentleness, took off with a butcher knife one day when two strolling squaws snatched some loaves of bread cooling in her window. The loaves were recovered. It could be dangerous for a woman to be home alone when her husband was seen leaving the farm. One brave woman carried on a conversation with an imaginary man, supposedly cleaning his rifle, until the eavesdropping marauders were frightened away.

Worst of all were the winters. Those three day blizzards, followed by intense cold, were death to travellers and to homes caught without their supply of firewood hauled from the river. (I remember that my father went to the Wild Rice River to bring home wood for burning every year.) In such storms, the oxen were the surest guides to find the way home through the blinding snow. Reishus told the story about when his sister became severely ill and the doctor in Minot was not available. Oxen were dispatched during a storm with a message tied to their horns to Uncle Torjus, the pastor, to come. He came to pray before she died.

Like all boys (and I was no exception), he admired cowboys. One of his most interesting stories was when three unbranded calves were missing from the farm. They had strayed off to a large cattle ranch just in time for the branding party. Young George decided that this was his opportunity to get to know some real cowboys and have some man-talk with them. While there, he decided to see if the missing calves were in the herd. But how could he tell? This would seem to be an impossible task, but not for George. He called out in Norwegian, "Kom Kjyra, Kom Kjyra," from the song "Seterjenten Sondag" (the "Chalet Girl's Sunday"), made popular by the famous Jenny Lind, the "Swedish Nightingale." Sure enough, three calves came bounding out and were released to him by the ranchers, despite their new brands. The calves understood Norwegian!

Education was irregular but critical to the pioneers. They realized that their lack of education was a great handicap. A group of 20 farmers organized in the winter of 1898 to start a school for themselves and hired George's father, Gunder, to be their teacher. They paid him $40 a month and helped with his chores on Saturdays. English was the top priority and "King's English" at that. History and citizenship also received top billing.

He told of waiting for hunting season at age 10. All summer long he had watched and protected a covey of prairie chickens. But when the

197

season opened, he had to shock grain. In desperation, he smuggled a shotgun and some shells into the field. Then he saw a buckboard coming with some hunters directly to his protected game. George met the invaders, took bead on one of their dogs and promised to blow its head off if they went after his chickens. They backed off after calling him some abusive names, including "a white-haired Swede." That was a nasty lie! He didn't have white hair and he was 100% Norwegian! George got his revenge years later when he cast the deciding vote against the man who maligned him at the election for the presidency of an oil company. There is a moral to this story. Treat children with respect. They could grow up to be your best friends. I count many of them as mine.

George grew up to be city auditor, a state legislator and active in selling insurance, machinery and clothing. His recollections are cleverly written with a good dose of humor. I wish I had known him.

CHAPTER 76

The 'Viking Battalion'
In World War II

ASECRET MEMO WAS SENT from the Headquarters of the Army Ground Forces at the Army War College in Washington, DC, to the Commanding General of the Second Army on July 10, 1942. It directed that a Norwegian battalion was to be organized from Norwegian nationals in the United States Army, or from Norwegian-Americans in the armed forces. It was to be called the 99th Infantry Battalion (Special).

Olaf Haaland of Carpio, North Dakota, for many years sheriff of Ward County, was one of the first dozen men to arrive at Camp Ripley, Minnesota, on Aug. 15 when the battalion was activated. It was the beginning of an exciting military career. Apart from combat ability, the main requirement for this group was the ability to speak and act like a Norwegian.

Originally, the battalion called for 931 men to be recruited from other army units for a secret mission. Though loyal Americans, these men had a special reason for interest in this assignment: they all felt a special love for Norway. I remember that day, April 9, 1940, when the Nazis invaded Norway and Denmark. Tensions ran high in many communities. The unthinkable act of Hitler's madness had happened. He had violated the neutrality of two peace-loving nations who had no hostile intent towards their neighbors. Now the Norwegian-Americans had a double reason for entering military service.

Already many Norwegians had found their way to America and were given automatic dual citizenship by joining the armed forces. Many had jumped ship since the merchant marine could not return to its homeland. Among them were shipbuilders, seamen, carpenters and cabinet makers. Joining them were farmers, cooks, college students and factory workers from the Middle West. They were transferred to Ft. Snelling in St. Paul, Minnesota, on Oct. 1. From there they went to Camp Hale, Colorado, on Dec. 19 where they underwent rigorous mountain training until Aug. 24, 1943. They learned to live on skis, carrying a 97-pound load. Everything they needed for survival was with them. Here they learned the value of "jeeps."

Their first overseas assignment was to Perham Downs, Wiltshire, in England, arriving on Sept. 16. They kept waiting for the command to be dropped by parachute into Norway. The Allied High Command decided that the planned attack on Norway would cost too many lives, so after spending some time in England and Wales, they suddenly shipped off for Normandy and the invasion of Europe on June 6, 1944, arriving five days later. There they joined other army units and fought in five major campaigns: Normandy, Northern France, Ardennes, Rhineland and Central Europe.

They were the first American troops to enter Belgium and fought valiantly in the Battle of the Bulge. Olaf Haaland was in charge of his platoon which included five tanks. Early one morning, while boarding his tank, he looked up at the GI giving him a hand and instantly recognized a neighbor from Carpio, Woodrow Anderson (now his wife's cousin). Woodrow had fought his way with the Army all the way up from North Africa. It was a good day! They spearheaded the advance of the troops and in a very short time took 1,200 prisoners. Later Olaf made contact with his brother, John, and joined him in Paris for three days of rest and recreation. These soldiers were so thoroughly Norwegian, Olaf told me, that they even gave battlefield commands in the Norwegian language.

On March 24, 1945, members of the 99th Battalion parachuted into Norway for sabotage missions and joined the underground for the liberation of the nation. Olaf, however, didn't make the jump because he had broken his leg playing volleyball. After the Nazis surrendered, the 99th Battalion was headquartered at Smestad, near Oslo, and served as Honor Guard for King Haakon and Crown Prince Olav. The men of the 99th Battalion also visited relatives and made new friends: by mid-September they had won the hearts of 87 young Norwegian girls who returned with them to America as their wives. They were deactivated at Camp Miles Standish in Boston on Nov. 11, 1945. A major with the 2nd Armored Division said of these men, "This Viking battalion is the only infantry that the tanks have trouble keeping up with."

The 99th wasn't the only force recruited for service in Norway. Wilfred Winters, a long time friend in Webster Groves (St. Louis), Missouri, was at an Army camp in Abilene, Texas, when he was recruited because of his Danish heritage for secret training that was to lead him to Norway. His assignment was to be a part of the group that was to destroy the heavy water plant in Rjukan, where Hitler was manufacturing deuterium-oxide for making the atomic bomb. Wil was sent to the University of Wisconsin in Madison for language study for six months. The group was suddenly disbanded as the Allied war planners decided to send Knut Haukelid and a detachment of Norwegians from England to do the job. Wil never made it to Norway, but he did get to Europe and after the war he visited his relatives in Denmark.

Forty-two years after the war ended, Olaf Haaland finally got to Norway. He and his wife visited their daughter, Joan, who was completing a doctoral dissertation in music in Norway for a degree at the University of Indiana. While there, they had an audience with Crown Prince Harald. Among the gifts they brought to the Royal Family was a copy of my book, *The Scandinavian Heritage*.

Scandinavian-Americans have retained a deep love for the lands of their ancestors while being loyal Americans. A strong spirit of comradery brings the 99th back for annual reunions. Of the 1,002 men who went to Europe, only 487 returned.

The 1989 Norsk Høstfest honored the "Viking Batallion" by inducting them into the Scandinavian-American Hall of Fame. A special medallion was struck for them. Long may they live!

CHAPTER 77

General Stuart Barstad —
Chief Air Force Padre

"SEEK PEACE AND PURSUE IT" was the theme emphasis in the United States Air Force Chaplaincy for 1988. Major General Stuart E. Barstad, Air Force Chief of Chaplains, addressed national Prayer Breakfast observance at Offutt AFB in Nebraska on the theme of "peace," and was asked: "Isn't that something like speaking against hand guns to the National Rifle Association?" "Not at all," he replied, "for peace is our profession."

General Barstad entered the Air Force Chaplaincy in July, 1955, following his graduation from Luther Theological Seminary in St. Paul, Minnesota. Intending to serve only one four-year term, he has seen service in England, Thailand, and twice at Ramstein in Germany. Stateside he has been stationed in New Jersey, Delaware, California, Texas, Colorado and Washington, DC. When the hostages held in Iran were released in January, 1981, Barstad was in Oslo, Norway, for a meeting with U.S. Ambassador Sidney Rand. He promptly flew to Wiesbaden, Germany, to meet the hostages and led a worship service for them. He became Chief of Air Force Chaplains in December, 1985.

A Norwegian-American from Colfax, Wisconsin, Barstad attended St. Olaf College where he wrestled and played varsity football. He had seriously considered being an athletic coach until the call of the ministry became too strong. He was given the Distingished Alumnus Award by St. Olaf at the 1989 Commencement.

Barstad believes that a major responsibility of chaplains is to help military personnel and top military leaders understand what the churches are saying. He feels that the issues of war, peace, and nuclear weapons are everybody's business, not just that of the military. He doesn't always agree, however, with what church leaders say about the military, and vice versa.

In November, 1984, Barstad addressed a Lutheran World Federation Consultation on "The Church and the Ideology of National Security" in Geneva, Switzerland. He admitted that he is sometimes embarrassed by the statements of some churchmen when they speak out on national security issues without having adequate information. He also said, "Military people make critical statements about the church or its leaders because they were speaking out on issues or questioning policies or decisions as they related to the moral and spiritual dimension of life." He concluded: "Neither approach enhances communication or speaks effectively to the real issues." In 1986 he participated in another consultation on the subject "The Church and the Struggle for Common Security" in Buckown, East Germany.

As the Chief of Air Force Chaplains, Barstad participated in the regular staff meetings of senior air force leadership at the Pentagon. He supervised 850 active-duty air force chaplains, about 600 reserve and national guard chaplains, 750 active-duty enlisted support personnel, and 250 reserve and national guard enlisted personnel.

The Chief Padre of the Air Force did a lot of preaching too. On Easter Sunday, 1987, Barstad addressed 6,000 people at the sunrise service at Arlington National Cemetery. He has also preached the baccalaureate sermon at the Air Force Academy in Colorado Springs, Colorado. He is a promoter of Bible study, having taught the *Bethel Bible Series* both at Vandenberg AFB in California and in Germany. He found his confirmation classes in Germany to be exciting because the confirmation service took place at the historic Trinity Church in Worms, the setting of Martin Luther's famous confession, "Here I stand."

While totally committed to the theme "Seek Peace and Pursue It," Barstad proudly wore the Air Force uniform as a military chaplain. He has received the Distinguished Service Medal, the Legion of Merit, the Meritorious Service Medal with three oak leaf clusters and the Air Force Commendation Medal. He also received the Robbe Louis Parris Hall of Heroes Gold Medallion from the Chapel of Four Chaplains in Philadelphia.

I first met Stu Barstad when we were students together at Luther Seminary in 1951-1952. We lived in the same dormitory. I was a senior while he was in his first year. I remember him even then as an exemplary person and a diligent student. I was in a position to know as I graded papers for two of the professors. We've renewed our acquaintance during the summers at Kabekona Lake near Walker, Minnesota, where we have both vacationed for many years.

In the early months of 1955, Lutherans were short 28 armed forces chaplains. I had the application forms for the Air Force when a strep throat condition seriously affected my speaking ability for many months. Dr. Gynther Storaasli, the Director of Lutheran Chaplains, advised me to wait with the physical exam until I was completely over the effects of the illness. During the school year 1955-1956, I took a leave of absence from the Mylo Parish to complete a Master of Theology degree. In the spring, the positions were filled and I returned to the parish to resume pastoral work. A year later, when I had begun a new pastorate at New Rockford, another Air Force commission was offered me. But then it was too late: I was committed to my new position. That's how close I came to being an Air Force chaplain. I've often wondered if the strep throat was divine intervention or a demonic obstruction.

Barstad accepted an Air Force commission in 1955 and remained at his post until his retirement in November, 1988. Now that he's retired from the military, Stu tells me that he and his wife, Ruth, want to attend the Norsk Høstfest in Minot.

Barstad sees the chaplain as somebody who stands in both the religious and secular worlds as "one who is deeply committed to the business of peacekeeping and peacemaking." He was responsible for publishing a booklet on the Air Force theme "Seek Peace and Pursue It" with some notable quotes. One from Eli Wiesel reads, "Our lives no longer belong to us alone; they belong to all those who need us." That, together with the quotation from the Sermon on the Mount, "Blessed are the peacemakers for they shall be called the children of God," sums up what Barstad believes about the role of military chaplains. We can be grateful for such noble leadership. The chaplains deserve our appreciation and cooperation.

CHAPTER 78

Sidney Anders Rand — Ambassador To Norway

VICE PRESIDENT WALTER MONDALE visited his ancestral home at Mundal in western Norway during Easter, 1979. To his surprise, he found 150 relatives. An idea occurred to him and upon his return to Washington he talked with President Carter about it. His request to the President was that if the post of ambassador to Norway should become vacant that someone from the Middle West with Norwegian roots be appointed to fill it.

Shortly thereafter the ambassador — Louis Lerner, a Chicago newspaper publisher — resigned because of illness. President Carter remembered his conversation with the Vice President and asked for a recommendation. After consulting with friends in Minnesota, Mondale called Dr. Sidney Anders Rand, President of St. Olaf College in Northfield, Minnesota, to ask if he might be interested in the assignment.

On Feb. 14, 1980 — after a security check by the State Department and the FBI, and a two-week briefing in Washington — Rand was sworn in as ambassador to Norway by Vice President Mondale. The ceremony took place at Boe Memorial Chapel on the St. Olaf Campus before an overflowing crowd of faculty and students.

The security check was thorough. Dr. Rand had to submit the names of 20 references plus the names of everyone who had lived within one block of him in Northfield for the past ten years. In addition, the government made up its own special list. Neither the interviewers nor those interviewed had any idea what it was all about, though there were some curious neighbors and townspeople.

The interview with the Senate Foreign Relations Committee was chaired by Sen. Frank Church. Sen. Jacob Javits, the vice chairman, was also present. They asked: "Mr. Rand, what makes you think you have the qualifications to be a U.S. Ambassador?" He answered that he had great confidence in his selectors and that his 25 years as a college president constituted a kind of diplomatic service. Sen. Jesse Helms asked:

"Do you speak the Norwegian language?" He replied: "Not as well as I should and not as well as I expect to speak it." With that brief interview, the Senators approved the appointment.

Three days after the swearing-in ceremony, the Rands were on their way to Oslo via Copenhagen. In his new job, Ambassador Rand reported to Robert Funseth, who was in charge of the State Department's relations with ten north European countries. The Undersecretary of State turned out to be Warren Christopher (originally Christopherson), a Norwegian-American whose roots were from Minnesota.

Once in Norway, there was a protocol for the presentation of Rand's credentials. First, he had to meet with His Majesty King Olav V. Then he called on the Prime Minister, the Foreign Minister, the Defense Minister and the other ministers of state. A call on the dean of foreign ambassadors was next. This was at the Embassy of the Soviet Union. The ambassadors of our NATO allies were visited next, followed by those of the other friendly aligned nations in Europe and then of the countries outside of Europe. The last group to be visited were the Warsaw Pact nations. There were four nations whose representatives the American ambassadors were to avoid except to exchange formal greetings at public functions. They were Cambodia, Cuba, North Korea and Vietnam, the reason being that the U.S. did not have diplomatic relations with them. Protocol specified a 20-30 minute time limit for these visits, with specific directions for seating of both ambassador and spouse.

What does an ambassador do besides attending formal functions? In Oslo, Ambassador Rand supervised a staff of 100. About half of these were Americans and the other half Norwegian nationals. Some Norwegians were advisors in such areas as agriculture and business, others served as chauffeurs, librarians, bookkeepers and photographers.

The Rands had time for private excursions too. They visited Mrs. Rand's relatives in the Trondheim and Hadeland areas. The ambassador found relatives of his mother at Sigdal in Numedal. That especially interested me since it's near Lyngdal, the home of my maternal grandfather. Rand's father's family had come from Surrey in England, though he has always been identified as a "Norwegian-American" during the many years that I have known him.

The Rands also took time to visit fairs, schools and churches. When we visited the American Lutheran Church in Oslo, the members were proud of the fact that the Rands had introduced the new *Lutheran Book of Worship* to them in 1980. Mrs. Rand was organist in the church during the time the Rands lived in Oslo.

The ambassador's residence is separate from the embassy, which is located on Drammensveien just west of Oslo's business district. The ambassador's residence, located on Nobelsgate, is a building of 24,000 square feet and is located about a mile west of the embassy near Bygdøy Alle. It is near Frogner Park, where the famous Vigeland statues are located. The embassy was secured by seven Marine guards, who carefully screened visitors. During the Rands' ambassadorship, there was one bomb threat and that proved to be false.

The Rands found that public demonstrations in Norway were carefully regulated by the police. Would-be demonstrators had to secure a permit a week in advance. Demonstrations were limited to one hour and had to be conducted across the street from the embassy. From his office window, Rand could watch the events without concern for violence. The demonstrations were generally quite peaceful and usually consisted of protests against nuclear arms or against U.S. policy in Central America.

The life of an ambassador is a busy one, with official duties taking up not only the work day but most evenings as well. Rand regularly met with the Norwegian Foreign Minister, delivering messages from the American President. His office also assisted tourists who had problems. Whenever Americans were jailed in Norway, the embassay had to report this fact to Washington and advise those who were detained as to how to get legal assistance.

Mrs. Rand (Lois) also found herself very busy. She directed the house staff, kept the calendar of events and made sure that groceries and other supplies were on hand for official functions. When there is a change of ambassadors, all perishable items are removed from the embassy residence and all new stock has to be purchased out of the ambassador's own bank account. For the ambassador to be reimbursed for expenses, at least 50% of the guests have to be non-Americans. Financial records had to be kept in both U.S. dollars and Norwegian kroner (crowns).

How did the Rands feel about their term in Oslo? They refer to it as a high point of their lives, although it cost them a considerable amount of their own money. They were amused by the fact that some Norwegians referred to the ambassador by his Norwegian-sounding middle name, "Anders," rather than by his English name, "Sidney."

The Norwegian government has twice given special recognition to Ambassador Rand's services in promoting good relations between our two countries. He has been awarded the Knight First Class - Order of St. Olav and the Commander of the Royal Norwegian Order of Merit. It is unusual for anyone to receive both awards.

I have known Dr. Rand since he was my teacher at Concordia College in 1945. It was my privilege to present him for induction at the Scandinavian-American Hall of Fame at the 1987 Høstfest. Vice President Mondale was also present to be inducted as well as to congratulate Ambassador Rand. It was a proud moment for me and for the Norsk Høstfest.

Ambassador Rand.

CHAPTER 79

The Hongs
Of Northfield

A FEW MILES TO THE SOUTHEAST of Wolford, North Dakota, a grain elevator bearing the name "Hong" used to mark the horizon's landscape. I knew almost everyone in the community from 1952-1957 while pastor of the Wolford Lutheran Church. I was surprised to learn that the grain elevator was named after the father of a famous Norwegian-American professor at St. Olaf College in Northfield, Minnesota, Dr. Howard Hong. (The elevator burned down in the mid 1960s.)

Howard Hong was born in Wolford on Oct. 19, 1912, but moved to Minnesota with his parents as an infant. I became acquainted with his uncle, Rev. George Nerison, who used to spend summers in Wolford during his retirement years. In his teens, Howard worked for Gamble-Robinson in Willmar, Minnesota, sorting vegetables and fruit. Earning a degree from St. Olaf College in the depth of the Great Depression (1934), Howard went on to study at Washington State, the British Museum and earned a PhD at the University of Minnesota in 1938. His list of achievements is too large for full comment in this story.

Edna Hong grew up in a Norwegian-American home at Thorpe, Wisconsin, and received a St. Olaf degree in 1938. She has had a distinguished career as a homemaker, translator, writer and lecturer. As a child, one of her jobs was to keep the woodbox filled. Out of those beginnings have come keen insights into life that she continues to impart.

The Hongs were featured in a book entitled *Growing Up in Minnesota*, in which ten writers reminisced about their childhoods, edited by Chester G. Anderson (University of Minnesota Press, 1976). In it the Hongs tell about their eight children (two of whom were adopted from Latvia). Howard was also a tree farmer. I remember friends who had attended St. Olaf telling me how the Hong's Northfield house was built around a tree.

They have not only been endowed with great talents, but the Hongs have been humanitarians. Howard was Field Secretary for War

Prisoners Aid of the United States, Scandinavia and Germany from 1943-1946. After the war, he was Senior Representative in Service to Refugees for the Lutheran World Federation in Germany and Austria (1947-1949), and served in a similar capacity for the World Council of Churches in Germany at the same time. In addition to his teaching at St. Olaf and travels, he also found time to lecture at Holden Village on Lake Chelan, Washington, during the summers of 1963-1970.

It was as a translator and interpreter of Søren Kierkegaard that the Hongs achieved special fame in the academic world. The Kierkegaard Library at St. Olaf College is named after Howard and Edna. It's a center for study and scholarly reflection. The space for the center is on the sixth floor of Holland Hall, an attic of a building patterned after the fortress monastery of Mont St. Michel on the coast of Normandy. Built in 1925, it became the architectural model for most buildings on the campus.

More than 7,500 books and other materials fill the library shelves, including their own personal collections of works by and about the famous Danish philosopher. One hundred sixty microfilm reels of Kierkegaard's manuscripts and papers from the Royal Library in Copenhagen are available to researchers. One file contains more than 3,000 articles, clippings, reviews, notes, and leaflets written about Kierkegaard, both during his lifetime and after. The Hongs presented the Library as a gift to St. Olaf College and it's open to all people of inquiring minds. Dr. C. Stephen Evans, Associate Professor of Philosophy at St. Olaf, is curator of the Library.

Howard started seriously studying Kierkegaard when a student of Prof. David F. Swenson at the University of Minnesota back in the 1930s. Swenson had a profound influence on future scholars through his teaching of Kierkegaard. When he died, his wife learned Danish so she could continue his work. Howard is now the general editor of the definitive 26-volume Princeton University Press edition of *Kierkegaard's Works*.

In 1983, the Hongs became the first recipients of the Minnesota Humanities Commission's annual Public Lecture Award. The award was to recognize Minnesotans who have "made significant contributons to the understanding of humanities." The citation reads: "The work of Edna H. and Howard V. Hong is exemplary in showing that the private lives of scholars and the public lives of stewards can be woven into whole lives of service on behalf of the humanities."

The first book I read by Edna Hong was *Muskego Boy*, published in 1944. I still regard it as one of the best children's books written. Another book by Edna, *Wild Blue Berries* (1987) is a mystery novel about a young pastor, Paul Amundson, which takes place on the north shore of Lake Superior. He discovered that his great-grandfather, Poul Amundson (1885-1912), and his great-grandmother, Margaret (1891-1912), had just begun their married life and church ministry in northern Minnesota when they both suddenly and mysteriously died. They had mistaken poison berries for blueberries. The strange part was that they knew the difference between the berries and yet met their fatal ends from the "Clintoni borealis," a blue-bead lily.

Four generations later, the young pastor discovered that their deaths were murders of revenge because his great-grandfather had not married one of the young women of his parish. To complicate it more, young Paul had arrived at the parish of his great-grandfather as a bachelor and fell in love with the great-granddaughter of the offending party. It's an exciting story how the tale unravels and the "curse" of the past deed had covered the descendants of this intrigue of jealousy. The book is especially interesting to those who want to learn some of the old Norwegian words that have been forgotten by most people today. It also has a good understanding of human nature and soul care.

The Hongs are also sensitive to the life situation for Native Americans. Edna's book *The Way of the Sacred Tree* (1982) gives a knowledgeable picture of American Indians, their wisdom, traditions and suffering. Howard discovered early in his life that much of the history written about the earliest Americans was neither honest nor respectful of their humanity.

Many honors have deservedly been given to the Hongs. Howard received the J. A. O. Preus Award for Humanitarian Service in 1953 and was named "Midwest Father of the Year" in 1954. Both Howard and Edna received Denmark's "Knight of the Order of Dannebrog" in 1978. In 1987, they received the Doctor of Humane Letters from Carleton College, the across town neighbor to St. Olaf, in addition to many other honorary degrees.

The best testimony to the Hongs, however, is what former St. Olaf students tell about them. Their home welcomed students for visiting and learned discussions. Their children grew up in an atmosphere of openness and charity. I admit to being impressed by my many seminary classmates who were St. Olaf grads. They received a quality liberal arts education at the feet of this learned, but unassuming, professor. Those are the best credentials any teacher could have.

Grain elevator.

CHAPTER 80

The Erickstad
Legacy

WHEN TOLLEF ERICKSTAD, his wife Brita Olson Aardal and their six children emigrated from Jølster, Norway, in 1883, they could not have realized what was in store for them in the New World. Neither could they have foreseen that a grandson, Ralph, would some day become the Chief Justice of the North Dakota Supreme Court. It's a long ways from the mountains of Norway's "Westlands" (west country) to the state capitol in Bismarck. Not many people are marked for such distinction.

Travelling with Tollef and his family were his brother Elias and family, his 16-year-old sister Andrea, Sam Overbo and his young bride, Anton Myklebust and Lars Knutson Klakegg. Boarding a steamer at the Bergen harbor, they landed at New York and travelled by train to Grafton, North Dakota, where Tollef had a brother, Gunder. Brita also had two brothers, Ole and Samuel Olson in Grafton.

The land at Grafton was already claimed. So Tollef and several other men drove a team of oxen pulling a wagon in search of land available for homestead. The sight of a cow following the wagon amazed the Indians in the Turtle Mountain area. They travelled as far east as the Mouse River near Minot. The soil met their approval, but they decided it would be better to settle nearer the railroad which had come only as far as Devils Lake. They found their future home near Starkweather, 25 miles northwest of Devils Lake and about 75 miles from their families in Grafton.

They must have wondered why they left Norway when they came to that treeless prairie of tall grass and sloughs in DeGroat Township. And just like back in Jolster, there were rocks in North Dakota too, though not as many. One of the agreements made with the government in getting land was that they had to plant trees. After breaking the tough prairie sod with the walking plow and building a house from available timber, they put up hay and returned to Grafton for work in the harvest fields.

213

In November they returned to their claim. The cow became so stiff from walking that she had to be loaded into the wagon. Before they reached their shelter, a severe snowstorm struck. The snowfall was so heavy that the oxen had to be led. A surprise awaited their arrival at the prairie shack — a skunk had taken up residence in their absence. The door and windows were still in the wagon among their winter supplies. The fuel for heating the shelter in the first winter was twisted prairie grass and buffalo chips. They roasted some of their seed wheat to use in place of coffee. (I remember how my father roasted cereal grains when I was a child when the coffee ran out and there was little or no money to buy any, even at 15 cents a pound.)

Before long, more people from Jølster arrived. It wasn't long before a schoolhouse was built which also served as a church. A congregation was organized in 1886 by Rev. Ole Aaberg, an enterprising missionary pastor to the Dakota Territory who lived in Devils Lake. In 1900 the first church was built and named after Aaberg's place of birth — Bergen in Norway.

This was a hardy breed of people. Tollef (1848-1927) and Brita (1845-1923) could have stayed in Norway since he was heir to the family farm. But he sold it when deciding to go to America. Their first home in the Starkweather community was a sod house.

Their son, John T. (1880-1958), was only three when the family came to America. After attending Aaberg's Academy in Devils Lake (founded by Pastor Aaberg) and a short course at the Agriculture College in Fargo, he married Anna Myklebust in Iola, Wisconsin, and returned to farm in the Starkweather community. He was also active as a County Commissioner and served as president of the Starkweather Telephone Company.

Their son, Ralph J., born in 1922, came from hardy stock. Those who knew him weren't surprised that his diligent habits for work and study would lead him to a successful professional career. He was one of six children, one whom died in infancy and another at age six. The prairie life took its toll and there were a lot of tears shed by these pioneer parents, as they lived with the uncertainties of life.

Ralph's career which led to the highest law position in the state came after a distinguished career of military service, study and law practice.

During World War II, he was a radio operator and gunner on a Liberator Bomber in the Eighth Air Force. After attending the University of North Dakota and graduating from the University of Minnesota Law School, Ralph began his work as an attorney in Devils Lake in 1949. He also served as the city Police Magistrate, the State's Attorney and was a State Senator when elected to the Supreme Court in 1962. While in the State Senate, he was often in leadership roles.

When I was the pastor of the Mylo Lutheran Parish, 65 miles northwest of Devils Lake from 1952-57, I became aware of this energetic young attorney in Devils Lake. When I moved to New Rockford in 1957, I got my first close-up glimpse of him. He spoke to our Kiwanis Club and impressed us all by his sincere and articulate presentation. I was not surprised when he became the Chief Justice in 1973 and was re-elected in 1978, 1983 and 1987.

Besides his judicial duties, Chief Justice Erickstad has served on many committees. He was president of the Executive Council of the National Conference of Chief Justices and of the National Center for State Courts. President Reagan appointed him to the Board of Directors of the State Justice Institute in 1987. Governor Sinner also presented him with the North Dakota National Leadership Award of Excellence in 1987.

Legal work is not the only thing that has occupied this busy Chief Justice's time. He has been active in the Boy Scouts of America and the YMCA. Both these organizations have recognized his leadership. The Boy Scouts awarded him the Silver Beaver Award and named the 1983 "Chief Justice Ralph J. Erickstad, Eagle Class" in his honor. The Missouri Valley Family YMCA presented him with the First Distinguished Service Award. The University of North Dakota honored him with the Sioux Award in 1973.

In June, 1988, Erickstad was given the Distinguished Service Award from the North Dakota State Bar Association. In May, 1989, he was awarded the National Center for State Courts "Distinguished Service Award" and was cited as "truly one of this nation's outstanding jurists."

There is another significant person in the Ralph Erickstad legacy. He was joined by Lois Jacobson of Minneapolis, a University of Minnesota graduate in business administration, at their marriage in 1949. They have two sons, John and Mark, both medical doctors in Bismarck. Lois

215

has achieved considerable fame for herself. Besides being an attentive mother and a supportive wife, she earned a Masters Degree in Public Administration at the University of North Dakota. She became the Vice President of the Western North Dakota Synod of the Evangelical Lutheran Church in America, in 1988, the first woman to hold this position. In the former denominations, this position was held by pastors. Mrs. Erickstad was one of 70 people who drew up the organizational plan for the ELCA. She has also been Chairperson of the Bismarck Park Board.

Chief Justice Erickstad addressed the Syttende Mai (17th of May) banquet for Minot's Sons of Norway Thor Lodge in 1988, in recognition of Norway's constitution of 1814. He spoke with his usual clarity of thoughts on the United States Constitution. He paid tribute to his Scandinavian heritage, but it was obvious that his first love and loyalty is to "the United States of America and to the constitution for which it stands." We have a better state because of the dedicated and wise judicial leadership of this grandson of the immigrants from Jølster whose first home in the New World was a sod house.

CHAPTER 81

Norman Borlaug And
The 'Green Revolution'

OR ABOUT TEN YEARS I flipped pancakes for the Annual Kiwanis Pancake Day in Minot. In addition to the usual fluffy white cakes served, some were made with a courser flour milled from "triticale." This is a cross between wheat and rye which was perfected by Dr. Norman Borlaug. It's the first man-made plant and has a higher protein content than plain wheat flour and can be grown on soils with marginal plant nutrition.

Borlaug is a hard-working scientist who was one of the pioneers of the "Green Revolution" and has been the Director of the Centro Internacional de Mejoramiento de Maiz y Trigo - CIMMYT (International Maize and Wheat Improvement Centre) in Mexico City.

On Oct. 20, 1970, Borlaug became a household name throughout the world. A reporter from Oslo called Mrs. Borlaug breaking the news that her husband was to receive the Nobel Peace Prize. Borlaug was out in the experimental fields training workers to continue the Green Revolution that the hungry of the world might have food. From that moment, he has belonged to the world.

Norman Borlaug was born March 25, 1914, on a farm near Saude in northeast Iowa, a few miles from the Minnesota border. His grandparents had been born in the Sognefjord area of western Norway. Grandpa Henry was particularly close to young Norman in his growing up years and told him, "Common sense, Norm, that's what the world needs. Education and common sense." These words have stuck in his memory all these years. His father, Nels, reinforced this counsel, "Education, Norm, puts vital power into a man. Fill your head now if you want to fill your belly later on."

His education began in a one-room grade school. We sometimes think that people who become famous must be unusually gifted with brilliant minds and hardly have to study. Borlaug has a brilliant mind but it wasn't all giftedness (sometimes that doesn't turn out to be a blessing).

With tenacious determination, Borlaug went to the University of Minnesota until he completed a PhD. While at the University, he met Margaret Gibson, a student whose family had originally come from Scotland. They were married in 1937.

When Borlaug graduated from eighth grade, the family held a conference to decide if he should go to high school. His second cousin, Sina, who had been his teacher, said, "No question! He's no great shakes as a scholar; his arithmetic is awful - but he sticks. He's got grit! High school will make him."

Borlaug didn't only crack the books. He was also active in sports. At Cresco high school, he was a star athlete in wrestling, football and baseball. At the University, besides waiting on tables and having a job through the National Youth Organization, Norman was a successful varsity wrestler. His determined spirit caught the attention of some of his teachers.

That tenacity stuck with him after earning a doctorate in forestry. He also studied agronomy. He first job was as a microbiologist with the Du Pont Company in Wilmington, Delaware. His life, however, was not destined to remain in the United States. The Rockefeller Foundation was requested by the White House to help the Mexican government develop its agricultural program and rescue its failing economy. Even though Borlaug had a position which was classifed as vital to the war effort, in 1944 he answered the call to work in Mexico.

It wouldn't be easy. It wasn't just that the Mexican soil had been eroding for generations, the problem was how to develop a short-stemmed, rust-resistant, wheat plant with high yield that would grow in both the tropical regions and the highlands of Mexico. It took years of hard scientific work to complete the job, plus convincing the farmers that this new way of growing wheat was a good thing. Many thought the new cereal grains would poison them. The agricultural scientists and politicians were often his greatest obstacles. To admit that Borlaug was right was to bring shame on themselves for having failed.

Many things have gone into successful agriculture. In an article co-authored with Christopher R. Dowswell entitled *World Revolution in Agriculture* in the 1988 Britannica Book of the Year, Borlaug lists the driving forces behind the spectacular production gains in agriculture.

He cites newly developed high-yielding crop varieties, increased reliance on irrigation and improved techniques for conserving moisture, chemical fertilizers, effective control of weeds, diseases and insects, and better farm machinery.

In January, 1976, Borlaug addressed a convocation at Wartburg College in Waverly, Iowa, on the topic: "Producing Food for Four Billion." Today, it's five billion. Borlaug sees the challenge both to produce more food and to educate people for population control.

Dr. Borlaug gave the first of the York Distinguished Lecturer Series at the University of Florida in 1985. It was a major address entitled "World Hunger: What to Do." In it he pointed out that it took 17 years (1943-1960) to enable Mexico to achieve self-sufficiency in food production. The statistics cited in the address are impressive. Wheat production in India increased from 11 million metric tons in 1966 to over 45 in 1984. Rice increased from 36 million metric tons in 1970 to 57 in 1983. Pakistan's wheat harvest increased from four million metric tons in 1966 to over 12 in 1983. China, he noted, had overtaken both the United States and the Soviet Union in wheat production, increasing from 22 million metric tons in 1965 to over 80 in 1983.

Borlaug is critical of government regulated economies which control food production, such as in the Soviet Union and most of the Communist countries. (It remains to be seen if Mikhail Gorbachev can change those policies.) Borlaug believes there needs to be private incentive with the government being friendly to the farmer so that prices can support production and that there is adequate storage in the event of crop failure.

As successful as the Green Revolution has been, the battle is not over. In his convocation address to the Punjab Agricultural University in 1987, Borlaug cited the urgent need for more people with scientific training to continue the research because plant diseases keep breaking through the defenses that scientists have built. To continue the work, Borlaug has trained more than 150 scientists from 23 countries.

Borlaug strongly disagrees with those who would restrict the use of chemical fertilizers and pesticides, and would do only organic farming. He calls this "confused science." He also defends the application of DDT when used properly. Borlaug was working at the Du Pont laboratories when DDT was first being tested. He has stated that only 25% of the earth's surface is land, and only 11% of that is suitable for agriculture. Since land is limited, the only way to produce more food, Borlaug insists, is to "increase the ability of existing crop lands to do the job."

As a result of India's increased production, my good friend Leo Holman (d. 1987), was in India and Punjab in 1969-1970 instructing the agricultural leaders how to store their bumper crops. Leo, then retired fom the United States Department of Agriculture and making his home in Minot, ND, made similar trips to Chile, Brazil and Taiwan. While still in the USDA service, he was one of eight specialists who travelled to the Soviet Union to improve their grain storage facilities. Unfortunately, the Soviet grain elevators were in such a sorry state that the officials wouldn't let the Americans make the inspections.

The Norsk Høstfest inducted Borlaug into the Scandinavian-American Hall of Fame in October, 1986. He addressed us with the hopeful message that we can conquer hunger if we want to badly enough. The scientific and technical skills are available, he claimed. He made a strong appeal for the attack on world hunger as a way to peace.

When I met Borlaug, his gentlemanly appearance didn't look like someone who had sloshed through mud in rice paddies, or worked tirelessly in the baking sun while trying to perfect a better grain, or who has argued down the heads of govenment to win his battle against hunger. Besides his work as a Consultant for CIMMYT, he is Distinguished Professor of International Agriculture at Texas A & M University. He has also been a Senior Scientist at the Rockefeller Foundation and was elected to the National Academy of Sciences. When the people of Mexico wanted to thank him with a gift of $5,000, he refused it saying, "I can't take this money. It's impossible for me to do that and still work here in this place."

A helpful biography is "Facing Starvation: Norman Borlaug and the Fight Against Hunger" by Lennard Bickel (1974). Bickel is one of the best known scientific writers in Australia. Dr. E. W. Mueller, former Director of CENCOAD (Center for Area Development) at Augustana College in Sioux Falls, SD, commented after reading the book, "It represents real progress."

Norman Borlaug And The 'Green Revolution'

"Norman Borlaug is one of the few enduring heroes of our wild, erupting age," wrote Vance Bourjaily, author of "Country Matters." I agree. Borlaug is a no-nonsense scientist committed to humanitarian goals. When the greatest heroes and events of the 20th century have been evaluated, Norman Borlaug and the Green Revolution are among the select few that deserve to be remembered. He manifests the best in the "Scandinavian spirit" of our times.

L. GAYLOR

The Green Revolution.

221

CHAPTER 82

Orion Samuelson —
'Voice Of American Agriculture'

"**A**FTER LIVING ON A FARM for my first 21 years, I got tired of getting up at 5:30 to milk cows. So I went off to school to become a radio announcer. Now I get up at 3:30." That's what Orion Samuelson, the "Voice of American Agriculture," told me.

You can listen to Samuelson as early as 4:50 a.m. (Central time) on the radio. Together with his associate, Max Armstrong, they broadcast 14 daily agri-business reports Monday through Saturday until 9:00 p.m. When I lived in Chicago, I heard him several times a day over WGN ("World's Greatest Newspaper" - the station is owned by the *Chicago Tribune*). This 50,000 watt Clear Channel station carries Samuelson's voice to millions of listeners.

Besides radio, WGN-TV brings Samuelson's "National Farm Report" to 300 radio stations. Besides radio broadcasting, Samuelson's "U.S. Farm Report" is telecast on 140 stations across the country, plus an additional 7000 cable systems in North America. His broadcasts reach out to 23-million homes.

Starting out in a one-room country grade school near Sparta, Wisconsin, Orion developed "Legg-Calve-Perthes" disease at age 14. This is an ailment in which the bone around the hip joint decays. During the first summer, he was in a body cast, flat on his back. He listened to Cub baseball games on WLS and decided to be a radio announcer. After two years of convalescing in a wheel chair and with crutches, he got his public speaking training through FFA.

In high school, Samuelson worked the public address system for basketball games. Then he entered the University of Wisconsin for radio training. They wanted to make a writer out of him. Orion said, "No, thanks," and went to Brown Institute in Minneapolis. After six months, he took a job at the Sparta station. He still had to get up at 5:30 and milk cows before going to work. Then he moved up to Appleton and

Green Bay. Big time - WGN in Chicago - came in 1960 when the station's regular farm broadcaster joined John F. Kennedy's Presidential campaign.

In 1975, Samuelson was elected Vice President of Continental Broadcasting Company, WGN's parent. He has been honored by almost every major farm organization in the nation. He's especially proud of his recognitions by the National 4-H and FFA. He is the only broadcaster to receive two "Oscars" in agriculture, one in radio and one in TV.

Travelling more than 65,000 miles per year, Samuelson's advice is often sought by U.S. Secretaries of Agriculture. In August 1983, he was with John Block as media observer when the U.S./U.S.S.R. Grain Agreement was signed in Moscow. He has also been to the Far East and Great Britain. He is a master of ceremonies for more than 100 meetings a year, including President Reagen's 1984 "Hometown Birthday Party" in Dixon, Illinois.

Samuelson has received many recognitions and awards during his career. He has been recognized by the American Soybean Association, the National Association of Soil & Water Conservation Districts, American Communicators in Education, the Dairy Nutrition Council, and was named "Chicagoan of the Year in Agriculture" by the Chicago Jaycees, besides being named National Farm broadcaster of the Year.

His foreign travels on behalf of agriculture have taken him to Scotland, England, Hungary, France, Denmark, Norway, Sweden, Austria, Canada, Mexico, Japan, Korea, Taiwan, Hong Kong, Philippines, Thailand, People's Republic of China and the U.S.S.R.

He is Vice Chairman of the Board of Directors of the Illinois Agricultural Leadership Foundation, a member of the Illinois State Fair Advisory Board and has been President of the National Association of Farm Broadcasters Foundations since 1975. He has also served on the Chicago Board of Trade and the FFA Foundation Sponsor Committee. It's difficult to measure his influence on agriculture except to say it has been outstanding.

Samuelson's interests are not limited to agriculture. He has been Chairman of the Board of Deacons for Trinity Lutheran Church in Evanston, Illinois, and served seven years on the Board of Governors for the Lutheran General Medical Center in Park Ridge, IL, when I was teaching there.

Minot's Norsk Høstfest Association honored this son of Norwegian immigrants by inducting him into the "Scandinavian-American Hall of Fame" in 1985. He represents the best in the Scandinavian heritage.

Orion Samuelson.

CHAPTER **83**

'Scoop' Jackson —
Counselor To Presidents

THE SEATTLE AREA BECAME HOME to large numbers of Norwegian immigrants. Among these was Peter Greset Isaaksen from Aure, west of Trondheim, and Marine Andersen from Norfold. Little could they have realized that their futures would be joined together in the New World and that their son, Henry, would become one of its most respected statesmen.

Like so many other immigrants, Peter did not retain any of his Norwegian names. Instead, he became "Jackson." The solid Scandinavian character of honesty and stubborn determination, however, became their trademarks as they began life in western Washington.

Henry Jackson was born May 31, 1912, in Everett, where he graduated from high school in 1930. The nickname "Scoop" was given to him by a sister because she thought he resembled a comic strip character by that name who always got others to do his work for him. He received a law degree from the University of Washington in 1935. The law office, however, was too quiet for this young Norseman. In 1938, he won his first election as prosecuting attorney. In 1940, he went to Congress as a Democrat and moved into the United States Senate in 1952, despite an Eisenhower landslide. He remained in that post until his death on September 1, 1983. He never lost an election.

When the Democrats were looking for a candidate to run against Nixon in 1972, his Senate colleagues picked him as the most qualified to be president. He didn't win the nomination, but he was highly respected by Kennedy, Johnson and Nixon who often asked his advice, particularly on matters of national defense. Kennedy chose Jackson as his running mate in 1960, but yielded to pressure for Lyndon Johnson in order to get southern votes. In 1968, he was Nixon's first choice for Secretary of Defense and was also offered the Secretary of State position. After serious deliberation, he turned down both offers.

Jackson took a hard line on Communism but believed in negotiations. He used his power to persuade the Soviets to soften their treatment of Jews. The presidents could always count on his support for defense. Together with his strong Americanism, he was also fiercely proud of his Norwegian heritage and showed his concern often for the well-being of Norway. People always knew where Jackson stood on issues. He was known to say, "I guess I'm just a stubborn Norwegian."

Jackson had a soft spot in his heart for the poor. He set up a fund to buy shoes for needy schoolchildren in his hometown. The money paid to him for speeches was used to provide scholarships for college students. No one knew where the money came from until the laws required public officials to make financial disclosures. He had never even told his staff.

On June 26, 1984, President Reagan posthumously awarded Jackson the Medal of Freedom in a Rose Garden ceremony. The president praised the senator from Washington as a protector of the nation, its freedoms and values. The epithet on his gravestone reads: "If you believe in the cause of freedom, then proclaim it, live it and protect it, for humanity's future depends upon it." All Americans can be proud of this Norseman from the West Coast. The world needs more of his kind.

CHAPTER 84

The American
Church In Oslo

A FTER WORLD WAR II, Norwegian-Americans sent money to Norway to rebuild and repair churches that had been destroyed during the war. It was also decided to build a church for an English speaking congregation as a "living monument" to remember the bond between the two nations.

"Look to the rock from which you were hewn" was the rallying cry in America as money was raised for the project. The words of Isaiah 51 were effective and on Oct. 12, 1958, Rev. Oscar C. Hanson of Minneapolis held the first service in rented space. The following spring, on April 23, 1959, a group of 83 Americans and Norwegians formed a congregation called "The American Lutheran Church in Oslo." It has become a spiritual home for people from all over the world. Church officials and dignitaries from both government and church in Norway attended.

The idea was first formulated in 1948 by Dr. Philip Dybvig, Director of Home Missions for the Evangelical Lutheran Church, a denomination with Norse roots. It took until 1956, however, before formal authorization was given at a church convention in Minneapolis. Pastor Hanson remained until 1960. Other pastors to serve the congregation were Dr. George Aus, a seminary professor from St. Paul (1960-62); Rev. Myrus Knutson of Los Angeles (1962-68); Rev. Arnold Nelson of Milwaukee (1967-1974); Rev. James Long of Houston (1974-1979); and the present pastor, Rev. Harry Cleven from Minnesota, who has been there since 1979.

A stately new building was dedicated on Oct. 11, 1964, at 17 Fritznersgate, near the entrance to Frogner Park, famous for its Vigeland sculptures. It was designed by the Sovik, Mathre and Mattson architectural firm of Northfield, Minnesota. The King's Guard trumpeters participated in the service. The Norwegian State Church has always been cordial to the congregation. It's an easy walk from the City Hall to the church.

We had our first look at the church in June 1977, but had to wait until September 1985 for an opportunity to be there on a Sunday morning. The service was preceded by Sunday school and an Adult Forum. I sensed a great deal of excitement by the members of their congregation. Following the service, almost everyone stayed to visit.

The most striking feature on the outside of the building is a large statue of "Christ the King" mounted on the wall. Designed by Egon Weiner of the Chicago Art Institute, it was dedicated by His Majesty King Olav V on August 27, 1967. The stained glass windows also add much to the building's beauty.

Some church members are permanent residents of Oslo, but many are transitory people attached to the NATO offices, embassies, and business firms. The new *Lutheran Book of Worship* used in America was introduced in 1980 by Dr. Sidney Rand, United States Ambassador to Norway, who had been president of St. Olaf College. Mrs. Rand was organist for the congregation.

If you are ever in Oslo on a Sunday morning, by all means visit this friendly congregation and join them for worship and "remember the rock from which you were hewn."

CHAPTER 85

'Høstfest' —
A Time For Celebration

"HØSTFEST" MEANS "FALL FESTIVAL" and is associated with the end of harvest. It is an ancient custom common to many lands. The Israelites annually celebrated three harvest festivals. The first was during the barley harvest in April. It took on a religious character known as "Passover." Seven weeks later when the wheat was gathered, they observed "Pentecost." The final festival came late in October when the fruit had been picked. It was called the "Feast of Tabernacles" or "Booths," as they pitched tents in the fields.

It is not surprising then that the Scandinavians also had festive gatherings when harvest was completed. Since the days of St. Olaf (d. 1030), Norway and its Nordic neighbors have had special prayers of thanksgiving for harvest time. This stands in stark contrast to the human sacrifices connected with their earlier pagan times.

The special prayer for Høstfest used in Norway during the immigration days began: "Almaegtige Gud, vor naadige Fader, du som oplater din haand og maetter alt levende med gode ting." Translated, this reads: "Almighty God, most merciful Father, who openest thy hand and satisfiest the desire of every living thing." It goes on to pray "for the living seed of Thy word sown in our hearts."

There are many Scandinavian festivals in America today. Among the best known are the Nordic Fest in Decorah, Iowa, and the Nordland Fest in Sioux Falls, South Dakota. The Scandinavian Day Picnic held at Vasa Park near Chicago is one of the newest. Some of the other areas where such gatherings are held include: Seattle, Washington; Detroit, Michigan; Topsfield, Maine; Solvang, California; and Spring Grove, Minnesota.

The Norsk Høstfest celebration in Minot, North Dakota, is unique. It began in 1978 and is held annually at the North Dakota State Fairgrounds. To the overwhelming surprise of the planners, over 5000 people attended the first year even though there had been only seven weeks time from the first committee meeting to the celebration.

It wasn't long before it was the fourth largest event in the state. In 1986, about 35,000 people celebrated Høstfest in Minot. The three larger events last over a week in contrast to the Høstfest's three days.

For the first Høstfest, local talent was recruited for entertainment. But within a short time, musicians even came from Norway and Sweden. A favorite at the event has been Myron Floren, said to be America's most popular accordionist. He quickly captivates the crowds with his easy stage manners and a few Norwegian words. The Minot Høstfest is held in mid-October, hopefully before the wintry winds begin to blow and when the farmers are done in the fields. Some of America's most popular entertainers have appeared at the Høstfest. These include Victor Borge, Burl Ives, Ray Price, Red Skelton, Mel Tillis, Anne Murray and Johnny Cash.

Not only has this Høstfest become the "premier Scandinavian event in North America, "as Chicago's *Vinland* newspaper described it, but it has received recognition in the highest circles of Norway. From the royal family down to the common people, the Høstfest has gotten attention.

To put on a celebration like this takes the skills and dedication of over 600 volunteers. Nothing but the weather can be left to chance. "Snow insurance" is a consideration to cover weather uncertainties. Among the many who have played key parts in this event, one person has provided the leadership that has made this event such a magnificent occasion. Chester Reiten, the president of a CBS affiliated radio and television broadcasting company, who was also a state senator and was for 14 years the mayor of Minot, has been president of the Norsk Høstfest Association since its beginning. He has made several trips to build ties between Minot and Skien, Norway, a city of similar size in Telemark. Each year, official visitors and friends travel between the cities with cultural exchange and to attend each other's celebrations. The Concert Choir of Minot State College has performed in the Skien church.

Visitors to the Høstfest come from all parts of the United States and western Canada. Many wear their "bunads" (local costume dress). There

230

is a queen contest, arts and crafts display, gift shops, food booths and musical entertainment. The Scandinavian-American Hall of Fame was established in 1984. It has inducted such famous persons as Col. Knut Haukelid, World War II Norwegian war hero; Orion Samuelson from WGN radio and television in Chicago; Carl Ben Eielson, famed Arctic aviator from Hatton, North Dakota; Brynhild Haugland of Minot who is the dean of state legislators in the USA; Jan Stenerud of football fame; and Nobel Peace Prize winner Norman Borlaug. One of the most stirring moments at the Høstfest is when the flags of each Scandinavian country plus the United States and Canada are presented and the national anthems sung.

Yvonne Ryding, Miss Sweden, was present as "Miss Universe" in 1984 and Hofi Karlsdottir, of Iceland, as "Miss World" in 1986. The "Hjemkommst," the Viking ship which crossed the Atlantic in 1983, has been displayed. A Norwegian worship service ("Høimessegudstjeneste"), using the liturgy of the immigrants at the beginning of the 20th century is held as the closing event on Sunday. The sermon in recent years has been in English since the third and fourth generations no longer speak or understand the Norwegian language well enough. Out of this ethnic celebration, the children of immigrants find resources of strength for their loyalty to the New World.

CHAPTER 86

'Maihaugen'
In Lillehammer

ONE OF THE MOST INTERESTING places to explore the Scandinavian heritage is at "Maihaugen," an open-air museum in Lillehammer. Situated on 90 acres, it was founded in 1887 by Anders Sandvig. Born in Romsdal and educated in Berlin, Sandvig moved to Lillehammer because of ill health. The area by Lake Mjøsen in southern Gudbrandsdal is highly regarded for its curative air.

I have seen several fine folk museums in Norway, but none excells the displays of Maihaugen. It has brought together an excellent collection of farms, a stave church, a school and workshops typical of the immigrant period.

The "Bjørnstad" farm had been owned by a wealthy family. The land was cleared during the Viking period (800-1066 A.D.). Twenty-six buildings make up the farm site: living houses, barns and sheds, granaries to store food for drought years and tool shops. There was no such thing as "going to town" to buy what was needed. They made it on the farm.

Two other farms are in the museum. "Ødegaarden" ("abandoned farm") had been vacant for over 300 years after the Black Death (1349). It has 17 buildings and is more modest than Bjørnstad. "Knutslykka," from north Fron, was built on marginal land. The farmers who lived there had to hire out to make even a meager living. These buildings resembled cotter's huts.

The "Garmo" Stave church has a special story. In 1021, King Olav, the "Saint," travelled through Gudbrandsdal to convert the people to Christianity. He gathered them for a meeting and said: "It would be a pity if such a beautiful settlement had to be burned." The king's custom was to first use gentle persuasion. If that failed, he threatened with fire and sword unless the people would be baptized. (The pagan kings gave no choices!) One of the converts was Torgeir the Old of Garmo in Lom. He was rewarded with a rich fishing lake in return for baptism and building a church. It was reconstructed in 1921 at Maihaugen with its beautiful stained wood carvings and a ship hanging from the ceiling. At the entrance are "stocks" where "sinners" were publicly punished for lawbreaking. It reminded me of Hawthorne's "Scarlet Letter."

The schoolhouse does not compare with today's excellent Norwegian facilities. But it was a significant step in popular education. The law which made confirmation necessary for civil rights also made schools a necessity. The Education Act of 1739 was a milestone for its time, but did not meet with popular approval. The farmers claimed that children were needed at home to work. In the Education Act of 1860, science, math and geography were added to the study of religion. This is when schools were moved out of homes into special buildings. The one room Maihaugen school building reminded me of Colfax School #5, known as the "Ista School," where I received my basic education in North Dakota.

A 10-day summer program called "Norwegian Roots" is held at Maihaugen. Besides the exhibitions, lectures, handicrafts, folklore and music, they have parades of costumes and guided tours. If interested, write: Norwegian Roots, Storgt. 56, N 2600 Lillehammer, Norway. If you attend, please tell me how you liked it.

CHAPTER 87

The Town Hall
In Oslo

OSLO HAS MANY PLACES OF BEAUTY. When I walk along Karl Johansgate, the street which leads from the palace to the parliament building, a good and strange feeling comes over me. It's where the Syttende Mai (17th of May) parade takes place each year. The pride of the city, however, is the "Radhus," (Town Hall), about three blocks south, across the highway from the harbor.

The Town Hall was opened on May 15, 1950, when Oslo celebrated its 900th anniversary. Thousands of tourists from all over the world come each year to gaze at its lofty ceilings and admire its famous art work.

The twin towered structure is built of red brick and stands where a permanent circus stood in the old days. Once there were a lot of tumbledown houses lining the harbor, but today it is a spectacle of beauty. It is to the credit of a former mayor, Hieronimus Heyerdahl, that the improvement project got underway. The work was approved in 1917 and a contest was held throughout Norway for ideas on the planning.

Architects were commissioned in 1920, but it took until September 4, 1931, before the foundation was laid. Many obstacles stood in the way. Norway had been an independent country only since 1905 and the world economy was in trouble. World War II brought everything to a halt. The building now houses the municipal offices and many of the nation's art treasures. The sculptures and paintings are worth taking time to see. They are massive and overwhelming.

King Harald Hardrade, who once led the Varangian Guard in Constantinople, protects one wall of the Radhus. The courtyard is flanked with scenes of the Old Norse Eddas (mythology).

The "Main Hall" is the showpiece of Oslo. The south wall shows Henrik Sorensen's mural of the nation at work and play. It's a panorama of Norwegian life. On the east wall is the "Occupation Frieze," showing the struggle for freedom from 1940-1945. Other scenes depict the "Labor Movement" and "The Commerce and Industry of the City."

I especially like the Corner Room with Edvard Munch's painting of "Life." Munch was an internationally recognized artist whose work shows deep emotion, often on the darker side. In the Festival Gallery, there are scenes from the different regions of Norway. It's hard to imagine how much variation there is in Norway's scenery and climate. In one respect, however, there is total agreement. This is found in a painting of His Majesty King Haakon VII in the Banquet Hall. Haakon VII was king from 1905 to 1958 and is the symbol of Norway's freedom.

The "Town Council Chamber" is designed in a semi-round with lightly stained modernistic furniture, surrounded by orange-red wood panelled walls. Behind the chairman's desk is a huge tapestry with more scenes of Norwegian life. Most touching of all is the decorated tree that stands in the City Hall during the Christmas season. The City Hall is a must for every visitor in Oslo to see. It's more than an office building. It embodies the spirit of freedom, held dear by Norwegians everywhere. Don't miss it if you visit Oslo.

Oslo City Hall.

CHAPTER 88

The Norwegian-American
Historical Association

THE IMMIGRANTS TO AMERICA were too busy clearing land, building barns and rearing families to think much about writing their history. It took 100 years before the Norwegian-Americans took that task seriously. Fortunately, a large number of newspapers were published by immigrants and some diaries were available. By the time of the immigration centennial in 1925, a large number of people who knew the oral history were still alive.

The Norwegian-American Historical Association (NAHA) was organized October 6, 1925. Faculty from Luther College in Decorah, Iowa, and St. Olaf College in Northfield, Minnesota, were the key organizers. These were a prestigious group of men who understood modern historical research as influenced by Frederick Jackson Turner and Charles A. Beard. They also understood the dynamics of environment and economics as decisive forces in history.

By the end of 1925, 200 persons had joined the organization. Growth through the years has not been spectacular, but steady. By the end of 1927, there were 842 members. The Great Depression cut into the membership. At the end of 1986, 62 years later, the Association had 1509 members.

I have been a member since 1979 and have been greatly impressed by the wide range and quality of its publications. Two major books a year are released. In 1986, I visited with Prof. Lloyd Hustvedt at the NAHA headquarters in the Rølvaag Memorial Library at St. Olaf College. He has been the Association's Secretary since 1959 and is Editor of its Newsletter. The chief researcher and writer is Prof. Odd S. Lovoll, a native of Norway. He works tirelessly to produce high quality writings. Prof. Lovoll recently wrote a history of Norwegian immigrants in Chicago entitled *A Century of Urban Life: The Norwegians in Chicago Before 1930*.

236

The reason why NAHA can function so well is the solid support of St. Olaf College. Dr. Sidney A. Rand, former President of St. Olaf and Ambassador to Norway during the Carter administration, was an enthusiastic promoter. He recruited me to membership. One of his goals was a chair in immigration history.

NAHA has had highly competent leadership since its beginnings. Theodore C. Blegen, professor of history and dean of the graduate school in the University of Minnesota, was the Association's managing editor from 1925 to 1960. Prof. Ole Rølvaag, author of *Giants in the Earth* and professor at St. Olaf was one of its founders and served as the first secretary until his death in 1931. J. A. Aasgaard served as president after he retired from the presidency of the Evangelical Lutheran Church (formerly Norwegian Lutheran Church in America) from 1954-1960. The list of leaders includes Ragnvald A. Nestos (1877-1942) of Minot who was governor of North Dakota from 1921-1924. Nestos was an effective recruiter of new members.

The Association was a sponsor of the Norwegian-American Historical Museum in Decorah, Iowa. Begun on the campus of Luther College in 1877, Prof. Knut Gjerset was curator of the museum from 1922 until his death in 1936. This work is carried on today by Vesterheim (Home in the West), an independent museum in Decorah.

The most visible work of NAHA is its publications. In the beginning, volumes were paperbound. But the decision was made to have future works hardbound so that they could be better preserved for future generations. Minot native Jon Wefald's *A Voice of Protest* (1971) launched a series of topical studies. It's a study of "Norwegians in American Politics" from 1890 to 1917. The new biographical series has published eight volumes. The series on *Norwegian-American Studies* is the place to look if you want to learn about pioneering in Alaska, Texas, Montana or most any other place Norwegians settled, or about controversial leaders such as Marcus Thrane or the great Telemark skier, Sondre Norheim. Its a goldmine for interesting reading. All of the contributing scholars have donated their research and writing.

A most illustrious volume, *The Promise of America* (1984) by Prof. Lovoll, tells the story of the Norwegian-American people. It's a companion to the exhibit featured in Norway during 1984 and the following year in America. The photographs of pioneer days alone are worth the price of the book. It was first published in Norway and then jointly in America by NAHA and the University of Minnesota Press. It's the best single volume that I've seen to tell the story of Norwegian immigration to America.

Interest in ethnic history is popular in our country now. The "melting pot" didn't completely melt. The Norwegian-American Historical Association deserves the interest and support of all ethnic Norwegians who want good information on their roots. The value of the publications received by members each year far exceeds the cost of membership. For information, write: Norwegian-American Historical Association, St. Olaf College, Northfield, Minnesota 55057.

CHAPTER 89

'Vesterheim' —
The Norwegian-American Museum

VESTERHEIM" - "WESTERN HOME" - is one of the oldest and most complete immigrant ethnic museums in America. Located in Decorah, Iowa, a Norwegian-American center since 1850, Vesterheim began collecting pioneer artifacts in 1877. "Western Home" stands in contrast to Europe as the "Eastern Home." Vesterheim began as a part of Luther College and became an independent corporation with its own national board of trustees in 1972.

Though I had known of this museum for many years, it was not until 1976 that I spent an afternoon viewing its acquisitions. Thirteen buildings make up the Vesterheim complex. The Main Museum Building is an elegant former three-story hotel built in 1877 and renovated in 1975.

Nine original buildings comprise the Outdoor Division of the Museum. The stone mill, important to the early farmers, sits on its original site and dates from 1951. The 17,000-square-foot Vesterheim Center, comparable in size to the Main Museum, was formerly a factory and warehouse built in the 1880s. It houses the Vesterheim offices, libraries, gift shop, classrooms, photographic and conservation laboratories, archives, exhibition galleries, woodworking shop, and volunteers' room. Between the Main Museum and the Vesterheim Center is the small Dayton Building, named after Silas Dayton, a merchant who constructed the building in the 1880s.

About seven miles from Decorah is located the Jacobson Farmstead on a ten-acre site. It was developed in the 1850s by the Jacobsons and remained in the family until donated to Vesterheim in 1977. Six buildings, standing on their original sites, document the culture of those rural immigrants who came to the Midwest almost 140 years ago. When fully restored, it will display Norwegian-American farm life at the turn of the century.

One unusual structure is the Washington Prairie Methodist Church built in the mid 1860s. A stone building that might be mistaken for a country schoolhouse, it stands on its original site near the Jacobson Farmstead in a well-preserved condition. The congregation was formed in 1852 by the Rev. O. P. Peterson, who later returned to Norway to organize the first Methodist congregation in his homeland.

Other buildings of the Vesterheim Complex include the Haugan house, a North Dakota prairie house and pumphouse, a Valdres house, the Tasa Drying house, the Egge-Koren house, a Norwegian Lutheran parochial school, the Norris Mille Stovewood house, the Mikkelson-Skree blacksmith shop and a Norwegian gristmill.

The Museum's collection includes more than 12,500 immigrant artifacts in addition to many books, manuscripts, phonograph records and tapes. The textiles and woodworking exhibits alone make a visit to Vesterheim worthwhile. I was especially impressed with the magnificent collection of trunks built in Norway. These have been restored, complete with beautiful rosemaling decorations.

The materials in the museum are limited to items made by Norwegian immigrants in America that show their ethnic background, objects brought from Norway which show ethnic heritage, and material which documents the early life of these pioneers. What is most impressive about Vesterheim is the quality of the exhibits. It makes one feel that many of the immigrants from Norway were highly skilled artisans who took great pride in their work.

His Majesty King Olav V of Norway serves as Honorary Chairman of Vesterheim's prestigious 74-member board of trustees. Among the board members are Ingrid Semmingsen of Oslo, one of the outstanding authorities on Norwegian immigration history; Gerhard B. Naeseth, the well-known genealogist from Madison, Wisconsin; Arthur E. Anderson III of Chicago, from the internationally famous accounting firm; Norman Lorentzsen, formerly Chairman of the Burlington Northern Board of Directors; and Mrs. Leif J. Sverdrup of St. Louis, who has given significant support to the preservation of Norwegian-American culture.

The Vesterheim Board of Directors set a $1,400,000 goal to strengthen Vesterheim's financial base, with $500,000 to be set aside as an endowment. Arley R. Bjella, former Chairman of Lutheran Brotherhood, was Honorary Chairman of the National Campaign, together with Walter F. Mondale, Norman E. Borlaug, David W. Preus, Sidney A. Rand, Eric

Sevareid, Jan Stenerud and many other nationally known persons of Norwegian-American heritage.

The Museum also publishes a quarterly illustrated newsletter which is sent to its 6,000 members; 24,000 people visit the Museum annually. Vesterheim also serves students from area grade and high schools as well as college and university students from Iowa, Minnesota and Wisconsin. It's open seven days a week.

Vesterheim also has pioneered a Genealogical Center in Madison, Wisconsin, directed by Gerhard B. Naeseth, which is planning a new facility to house its work of assisting Norwegian-Americans to trace their family roots. It has been called the "premier Norwegian-American genealogy organization in this country." They need $350,000 to reach their goal.

Naeseth has been the leader behind Vesterheim's most recent development. He was on the staff of the University of Michigan for six years, Oklahoma State University for eight years and the University of Wisconsin for 30 years until his retirement in 1978. Since then, he has volunteered his time in the development of this valuable Vesterheim endeavor. He is preparing a five-volume *Biographical Dictionary of Norwegian Immigrants Prior to 1851*. Naeseth has also been awarded the Knight's Cross, First Class and the Royal Order of St. Olaf.

The Vesterheim Board of Directors held its 1987 meeting in Minot during the annual Norsk Høstfest in October. Vesterheim is impressive. It deserves the attention and support of everyone who wishes to keep the best of the Scandinavian spirit alive in the New World. It serves well the 6 million living Americans who claim this ethnic background. For more information, write: Vesterheim, 502 W. Water, Decorah, Iowa 52101.